By Divine Design

by
Michael Pearl

Published by
The Church AT Cane Creek
1000 Pearl Road
Pleasantville, TN 37033
United States of America

> All Scripture quotations taken from the
> # King James Holy Bible

Until now, all that I have published was written to answer a need in my readers. By Divine Design was written to answer a need in the author—a need to speak, to document my world view. Forty years of study, reflection, interaction, and teaching has developed a perspective that, though not original in any single point, is unique as each individual is unique.

If you were to join this author on the front porch to spend the afternoon discussing the great issues that have historically been of deepest concern to all mankind, you would hear much of the content of this book.

Molded by Scripture, prayer, meditation, interaction with saints and sinners, the joyful and the suffering, the learned scholar and the common man, a philosophy is forged. I give you mine. You be the judge of its truthfulness.

My regret is that your side of the discussion is missing. Many of you will not agree with some of my views. I have debated with many a theology book and argued a thousand different world views. My thoughts have been sifted and will continue to be so. Possibly this little publication will help you sift your own views.

My thanks goes to the many inmates incarcerated in CCA at Clifton, Tennessee. It is at their urging that I finally decided to commit this manuscript to publication. Pre-publication copies circulated among them caused such a stir of excitement and brought forth testimonies of blessings that after four years I decided to go forward with printing.

Let us judge all that we believe according to the Scripture and all that we are according to the Spirit of God.

Michael Pearl

CONTENTS

Preface

Unrestrained human will, sovereignly permitted, appears to have grown into a malignancy, for we fight and kill to be free only to succumb to a bondage within. Our inner captivity seems to be so thorough as to be the first principle of existence. Yet we resist our degradation like a man resists drowning, for when we fail to be good we pretend to be.

When we find ourselves unfulfilled, even miserable, we look to religion or philosophy. Diversity of philosophy testifies to our agreement that there is a problem. Diversity of religion testifies to our lack of agreement on the solution. Philosophy sits on the steps explaining the process, watching the captives march off to their cruel destiny, while religion, far from being a solution, is often leading the captives. In the end the philosopher cowers alone, harmlessly babbling his imaginations, while the priest takes the sword to make converts. So the Holy Grail is often stirred with a bloody dagger.

Historians stand over the graves of great men to record their achievements. Regardless of our pomp and glory, disease and death is the door through which we all must exit. The feeble moth and decay eventually erase all evidence of our passing.

Are we actors in a Shakespearean tragedy? Is earth a stage on which we perform a pre-written drama? It is as if we began our existence somewhere in the middle of a play and will disappear beyond the curtain long before the last act. Without a script the performance has no meaning beyond immediate personal indulgence.

Sometimes in the midst of the pain and injustice, when it becomes obvious there is no fairness, some are prone to doubt that this "drama" has any plot. Theories of self-creation and chance have replaced belief in an intelligent Creator. Belief in an unplanned existence without destination begets meaninglessness, which begets futility, and futility begets loneliness. It has been observed, unless earth's inhabitants are indulging they are all lonely.

Many doubt God's good intentions, angry at the Deity whom they feel is responsible for their sufferings. While denying or at least ignoring His existence they continue to blame Him for not being more in control. Their concern is not so much with overall meaning as with their own fulfillment.

> "Why did He do this to ME? If this God knows what will happen in the future, He would have known the results of His botched creation." A baby dies... "Why did God let this happen?" An accident, and someone is left crippled or scarred... "Doesn't God care?" War, famine, AIDS... "If I were God, I would ...," and so it goes. Very few of earth's inhabitants ever really trust their Creator.

Inmates in the state prisons, students on college campuses, and our neighbors next door all ask the same accusing questions. Likewise, Christian parents standing beside a small grave are often heard challenging God. If we fault others for questioning God, we should be reminded that our heart often asks questions our lips are too cautious to speak.

- "How can I believe and trust a *'sovereign God'* who allows so much evil? Is God impotent? If not, then does He care?"

- "Why did God even make us capable of sinning? If He knows all and is all powerful, couldn't He have created a world without sin and death?"

- "Why? Why did God create Lucifer if He knew it would result in sin?"

- "Why did God put the *tree of knowledge of good and evil* in the garden if He did not want Adam and Eve to sin?"

- "If I could help it, I would not allow my children to be subject to pain and suffering. Why would the Creator let souls live forever in Hell? Why would He not just destroy them so they would not continue to suffer?"

- "Couldn't an all-wise God develop a plan that didn't involve suffering for so many?"

Theologians often dismiss these questions by answering, "God didn't create sin, Satan did," or saying, "God doesn't send men to Hell, they send themselves by their sin." Why do these answers not satisfy our deepest sense of the rational?

On many of these difficult questions God has chosen to remain mostly silent. When challenged, "Why have you made me thus?"

His response has been, *"Shall the thing formed say to him that formed it, Why hast thou made me thus? Hath not the potter power over the clay?"* Apparently God does not think that a clinical analysis of His motives or an apologetic defense of His actions is necessary to vindicate His moral government; for God *"giveth not account of any of his matters."* Just as wise and noble men do not stoop to defend themselves before cynics and petty critics but remain "presidential," so also in the face of human criticism, God has remained Godly.

God has chosen to be silent and remain above the fray, so I may be presumptuous as I come to His unsolicited defense. Nonetheless, I will take up the answer that Elihu directed to Job: *"Suffer me a little, and I will shew thee that I have yet to speak on God's behalf. I will fetch my knowledge from afar, and will ascribe righteousness to my Maker (Job 36:2-3)."*

Chapter One
Before The Beginning

"In the beginning God..." That was before—before time. It was eternity past; and yet, being before time there was no eternity and no past, nor any future. No dimension to contain empty space. Nothing moved, nothing breathed. There was no color or odor—nothing to see and no eyes to see it. There were no physical laws because there was nothing physical to govern. No up or down; no in or out; no coming or going.

In timelessness God existed alone with Himself. He is They, and They are He. He is one, yet the One is three, and the Three are one. He communed with Himself as God entered counsel together.... Language is inadequate.

Math did not yet exist; still today it fails us in defining the Godhead. God can no more be counted than He can be contained. There was nothing outside of God, nothing distinct from Him. All was God, and God was all—singular unity. If it were not for God's capacity to fellowship within Himself, He would have been lonely.

"In Him is life." Life is never static. It begets. God in counsel with Himself set in motion His "life's work." The raw material for creation came from within God Himself. God acting is energy. Energy formed is matter. By so willing, He stretched out nothing into dimension and laid it all at the beginning of an endless line which came to be called *time*. With His word the only tool, His energy was flung against the canvas of void space, and matter was the repercussion. Physical nature began.

Physical creation

At this point all of creation was under the absolute, pre-programmed control of God. It was mechanical—fixed to precise innate laws. The physical universe did not have the capacity to make choices. All turns of events were the direct act of God. There was no possibility of anything violating His will. No will existed outside His own.

God had created a limited number of elements comprising innumerable molecules formed into a variety of substances. This vast physical expanse, separate from its Creator, had no capacity to think, feel, or will its destiny. The physical creation does not have the potential to grieve God. It will never surprise Him or disappoint Him. There is no love given and none received. Like a grandfather clock the universe had its bounds fixed at its creation. It will always be exactly what it was created to be until it wears out. God can continue to sustain nature, alter or destroy it altogether without having to be emotionally involved. Not being endowed with human qualities, like self-consciousness, physical nature can be dismissed as a farmer plows under a field of grass to make room for another crop. Physical nature will never be good or bad. It will never love or hate. It will never be blamed, nor will it feel shame. In brief, the material universe lacks personhood.

A self portrait

The beauty and complexity of the physical world did not satisfy God's ultimate intention. What He did next appears daring. From our perspective it looks as if He took a risk. Maybe we should say He exercised faith. As artists seek to express themselves through rendering images of their external world, so God fashioned an image of the only external reality, a tiny reflection of His own person, a mini-sculpture in His own image. God formed a living self-portrait. Desiring to extend His own self-consciousness, He formed a *being* who, like Himself, would stand completely apart from nature, above all other creation.

In the lower parts of the earth, as from the womb of God, the Creator molded the particles of matter into a suitable vessel. Then came the "leap of faith." From deep within, God exhaled

His own self-perpetuating life into the vessel of clay. Physical nature was linked to human soul, infused with Divine breath, and an eternal, independent person was born, a son of God. Thus began the parallel human and Divine journeys merging with our present.

Independence

When God gave way to self-expression, generating the human race, He was duplicating His own independent personhood. Therefore, when He exhaled His breath into Adam's lungs it was the end of the Creator's control. God stepped back, and before Him stood a creature made of the essence of God, an independent, self-determining, personal soul, distinct from all others, including God. As such, neither these created beings nor their descendants can ever be obliterated. The Creator had "transplanted" Himself, and the "plant" carried the essence of unending life. This first human soul was only a seedling wrapped in a shell of flesh, but it was destined to mature into the likeness of its Creator.

Just as a mother releases a child from her womb to become a wholly distinct and separate being, so God had cut the cord of Divine control and released Adam to his own individuality. The Creator was reproducing His infinite-God self on a finite-god level. God desired a family, sons and daughters, brothers and sisters, peers, persons with whom He could experience social parity. No aspect of nature could answer His designs for family and community. Personhood was His goal. Nothing short of a personal soul in God's own image could fulfill this self-imposed need. In forming this independent soul and then releasing him to his own cognizance, in a real sense, God had entrusted His sovereignty to this man and his descendants. This and all that would result from it were and are by Divine design.

Chapter Two
In His Image

Reasoning from the finite to the infinite

"And God said, Let us make man in our image, after our likeness (Genesis 1:26)." Obviously, the image of God in which we were created could not be physical; it must be metaphysical—soul and spirit. This knowledge that the soul of man is an offspring of the soul of God opens a window for us to understand God as well as ourselves. The Creator may have hidden Himself, but he left behind a witness as to His nature. Since an image is a mini-replica of the original, to know something of our own nature is to know something of Him who created our nature after His. While He is infinite and we are finite, a seemingly incomparable difference, we can nonetheless reason from the finite to the infinite. By ascertaining our own attributes and then projecting them into infinity we get a picture, however vague, of the original prototype.

One may reason that human depravity leaves the human image too marred to be of any value in understanding the nature of a holy God. Yet, does not an archaeologist take a few marred fragments of ancient pottery and reconstruct the original? Furthermore, the depravity of a thing (departure from its original purpose) does not obscure the original image; on the contrary, it defines that image by its very departure from the obvious inherent pattern. When we know we are seeing the original through a process of degeneration, accordingly we can make adjustments in our perception of the original image. Depravity is easy to detect in its departure from the order and perfection of the original state.

The depravity of the race is not a depravity of original image but of the use made of that image. When the Bible speaks of the image of God it is not a statement of how man acts but of his constitution—the structure of human soul. The attributes of human soul remain the same whether employed honorably or misused. We will discuss the composition of human soul directly.

But first, lest one be carried away with the thought that natural man reflects a Divine origin, let it be understood that when we look at humanity and say we see the image of God, we are like a child pointing at the surface of the water in a mud hole and exclaiming, "Look! I see the sky."

In His likeness

If God would have persons with whom He can share common interests, they must of necessity be made similar to Him. God and man (also, the angels and other created personalities) are the exact same in kind, though vastly different in degree. Just as a 50-watt radio transmitter-receiver can communicate with a 50,000-watt transmitter-receiver, because they are exactly of the same kind (nature), though greatly different in degree, so God and man can communicate. The human soul, reflecting the infinite person of God, can only be accounted for by the soul of God.

Triune Being

All creation bears the stamp of its Creator. Both the physical and the metaphysical world demonstrate an inherent design and therefore reveal a common designer. The similarity of design suggests a purpose and confirms that nothing came about arbitrarily.

The nature of God is the pattern for all that is created, material and non-material alike. The Bible represents the one God as a triune being. This is a strange concept that one is three and three are one until we see this very enigma represented in the creation, which creation, as we have said, reflects the nature of the Creator. Creation is so thoroughly stamped with God's triune *likeness* that the apostle Paul was able to tell us that the Godhead is clearly visible through natural creation.

The atom, once thought to be the smallest part of any substance, is three parts: protons, neutrons, and electrons. But now it is know that the protons and neutrons at the center of the atom are composed of three quarks each. And according to the most current model, scientists are puzzled as to why there are just three generations of leptons and quarks, no more or less.

Time is threefold: past, present, and future. Our world has three kingdoms: animal, vegetable, and mineral. Life on planet earth is divided into three main branches: bacteria, archaea, and eukaryotes. The sun, a symbol of God, emits alpha, beta, and gamma rays. There are three basic elements in soil, causing a plant to grow: nitrogen, phosphorous, and potash. There are three primary colors (pigment) from which all other colors are derived: red, yellow, and blue.

Like our triune Creator, we are a triune being: body, soul, and spirit. The body consists of flesh, bone, and blood. The flesh has three layers of skin: the Epidermis, the Dermis, and the Subcutaneous tissue. Our blood solids consist of three main cells: platelets, red cells, and white cells. Our nonmaterial self (the soul) is mind, will, and emotions. In the emotions, we can love, hate, or be indifferent. Human capability is thought, word, and deed. Logical thought, the activity of the mind, demands a major premise, a minor premise, and a conclusion.

All this reflects the image of God who is revealed to us as a triune, singular being: Father, Son, and Holy Spirit. Within the Godhead are the Lover, the Loved, and the Spirit of Love. God is a personal soul manifesting mind, will, and emotions—the same *"yesterday, today, and forever."*

As God's persons are three, His attributes are three: omniscience, omnipresence, and omnipotence. All creation is designed after the *"likeness"* of those attributes. Based on God's nature, space is three-dimensional: height, width, and depth. As each dimension is separate and distinct, yet each exists within the other, and all three dimensions are essential to the concept of space, so God is Father, Son, and Holy Spirit, distinctly different, inseparable, and in combination comprising the one infinite God. God is not three parts or three different manifestations. He is one essence, composed of three interdependent persons, each essential to the whole and each containing and expressing the whole of the Godhead.

Space, created after the infinity of God, is the physical expression to His infinite omnipresence (being everywhere). Infinity is conceptually present in the combined three dimensions. Each dimension unendingly projects toward infinity, and together the three dimensions project into infinity in every conceivable direction, just as do the infinite attributes of God.

- The likeness of God's omnipresence is reflected in our own soul, as seen in our ability to move about within three-dimensional space.

- The likeness of God's omniscience (knows everything) is reflected in our gift of knowing and our ability to increase in knowledge.

- The likeness of God's omnipotence (all-powerful) is reflected in our inherent ability to exercise creative power within our own environment.

The three attributes of the soul (mind, will, and emotions) are also interdependent. Like unto the triune nature of its mentor, the existence of any single soulish attribute implies and necessitates the others. One cannot rightly conceive of mind without will. A mind without a will could not think an original thought, or change thoughts, or even maintain continuity of thought. It is also inconceivable that a man could entertain an idea, value it, will it to come to pass and not *feel* in accordance to its advancement. Feelings (emotions) are an inevitable result of valuing something—which is the mind choosing. To negate the concept of either the mind, the will, or the emotions would render the other two attributes inconceivable. They exist as one concept—soul.

The history of man is a chronicle of his struggle *to know* (an image and likeness of omniscience), *to go* (an image and likeness of omnipresence), and *to do* (an image and likeness of omnipotence). Unquestionably, God's triune attributes continue to be reflected in all of creation.

The breath of life

The Soul of Man: All breathing creatures have a soul. But of earthly creatures, only man has a spirit-soul (called *living soul* in Gen. 2:7). Souls of dissimilar creatures obviously differ from each other in degree of sophistication, and of all earthly creatures we humans are endowed with the highest soulish attributes. But if our differences from the animal kingdom were only a matter of degree, say a higher intellect, we would still not be persons. Only one attribute sets us not just above but apart from other animal kind: God's own spirit breathed into us at creation. That spirit imparts to our souls the attributes of self-consciousness and self-determination. It completes the *"image and likeness"* of God.

The three essential aspects of our person correspond to the godhead. The soul of man corresponds to God the Father; the spirit of man corresponds to the Holy Spirit; and the body of man corresponds to Jesus. As Jesus is the only aspect of God that is visible, so the body is all that is visible of man. We are truly in God's *"likeness."*

The Spirit of Man: One word of clarification: The spirit given to the human race through Adam is not the person of the Holy Spirit. It is the essence of life itself, that life which is common to the Godhead. Humanity shares personhood with God by sharing mind, will, and emotions infused with the *spirit of life*. The spirit breathed into Adam became Adam's own spirit, separate from God. It is the presence of that eternal spirit that makes the soul alive and man immortal. All who are conceived are made alive by that spirit, and therefore can never be destroyed. The triune soul fused with the spirit is essential to human personhood.

God is
God not
us
look in
Bible
God
reigns

Chapter Three
The First Man

Moral children

As Adam rose from the dust he was physically complete but morally undeveloped; he was yet without moral consciousness. The original couple drew their first breath, saw their first sight, and spoke their first words in absolute innocence. They were without sin, but they were also without righteousness, without character. Morally they were neither good nor bad. Each of their adult bodies housed a moral baby. They had no knowledge of, or experience in, right and wrong.

Different from infants, their moral capacity was mature, but like infants they were at the very beginning of moral understanding. The understanding and discernment that comes with experience was not yet theirs. They were naive. They had no wisdom. Their moral character was all in the future, yet to be decided. They were in adult bodies when only one minute old. They were aged, with no past. They were each a published book, the first half just blank pages—the latter half yet to be written. Like an unlit candle their consciences awaited the exercise of their wills.

Like children, their growing souls were wrapped in mortal bodies of weak flesh, bodies that craved indulgence. They were endowed with passions that would eventually lead their souls into crossroads of conflict with the flesh. God preempted that hour of temptation by arranging an artificial trial. Perhaps the purpose of arranging the temptation in this controlled environment was to provide them with well defined boundaries. Being moral infants, they needed guidance and direction.

As one might do with a child whom he sought to instill with restraint and self-discipline, God placed a forbidden tree in the

middle of their paradise. There was nothing inherently evil about
the tree, but by the attachment of a command to it this otherwise
ordinary tree became a moral training ground. If the heavenly
Father had been concerned for the preservation of the tree He
could have placed it "out of sight and out of mind." But instead,
He placed it right in the middle of the garden where they would
frequently pass. It was a place that presented a daily opportunity
to exercise and develop their moral natures.

Adam and Eve had moral potential but no knowledge or
experience apart from that tree. There was no other opportunity
to be tested. To develop positive moral character, one must be
tested. God designed life to be a spiritual womb, a place where
the work of creation is brought to maturity. The physical creation
is complete and He is rested from it, but the moral creation
continues. Men are not born wise, righteous, experienced, or
developed in consciousness of duty. This can only come about
through the risks of personal experience.

Temptation

When God placed Adam and Eve in the garden, He did not just
drop them off in a paradise of leisure to live a life of indulgence.
They were given a mini value-system: *"Eat of all the trees, but
don't eat of the fruit of the tree in the midst of the garden."* They
could be tempted in three ways only:

- Through a desire to satisfy their appetite.
- Through a desire to satisfy their sight by its loveliness.
- Through a desire to be immediately wise in the knowledge
  of good and evil.

The first pull of temptation came through the sight of the eyes;
the fruit was "lovely." A deepening of the temptation occurred in
the imagination—conceiving the taste of its fruit to be very
desirable. The final aspect of temptation was a lie coming from
one who represented himself as: one of the gods, professor of
higher learning, revealer of deep secrets, imparter of wisdom, a
friend to point out the good life. He persuaded, *"Ye shall be as
gods, knowing good and evil."*

The presence of this tree and the command not to eat was,
compared to our present environment, a minor source of

temptation. If they had been induced to eat through extreme hunger, or if their sight had been challenged by something unusually pleasant to the eyes, or if knowledge and wisdom had been otherwise forbidden—if any condition had been prevalent which left them with severely inflamed passions—then we might sympathize with their yielding. But this was not the case. They were like children placed in a room with a hundred interesting toys and permission to play with all but the one on the shelf. Very few children will handle three of the toys before turning to the one on the shelf. To a naive, inexperienced child, the forbidden becomes more desirable. "What is the secret of the toy on the shelf? What do the adults know that I don't? I will be like an adult if I have access to that toy, for it is forbidden to children."

The child could expend all of his passions on the other toys, and in time he would become an adult, knowing the secrets of the forbidden toy. But he must have it now. It would taste good—children put toys in their mouths. It is pleasant to the eyes. And, "I will be wise like one of the big people if I possess that toy *(knowledge of good and evil)*."

At the point when passions are calling, the only thing that can restrain the child is an overriding faith in, and respect for, the word of the adult who gave the command. It is a crossroads of either obedience based on faith or of personal indulgence.

Sight of the eyes

As Eve beheld the tree, she was deceived by its sheer loveliness. It was *"pleasant to the eyes."* The sight of her eyes led her to begin to function on a purely sensual level. Since it was God who gave Adam and Eve sight and a desire to view things pleasant, there could be nothing sinful in the sight itself. It is when she allowed sight to take precedence over intellect that sight led to inordinate indulgence.

Likewise Satan tempted Christ by showing Him *"the kingdoms of the world and the glory of them."* The sight of His eyes led Jesus to be tempted to achieve, in an inappropriate manner, the very end for which God had sent him into the world. He came into the world to be king, and here Satan was offering it to Him. If he had not desired that kingdom there would have been nothing tempting about the offer.

If every sin were garbed in ugliness, there would be no temptation. If we were offered something for which we had no appetite, again, it would not be tempting. *"Every man is tempted when he is drawn away of his own lust, and enticed (James 1:14)."*

Satan did not create the sight of the eyes, nor does he create anything lovely. He just devises ways of abusing Divinely given sight.

Appetite

Eve was also tempted through her appetite for food. But similar temptations can come to us though any of our bodily passions. Lust for food has proven to be more powerful than passions for either sex or survival. Men will forget sex and risk their lives just to get something to eat.

God created our bodies to be dependent upon food. And if we go without food for very long, the need to eat becomes a driving passion. Jesus Himself, while suffering hunger, was tempted to turn a stone into bread, satisfying His natural appetite. As with the human race, Christ could only be tempted in this manner because of the God-given appetite for food (and in His case, hunger was compounded by forty days of fasting). There is nothing evil in appetite itself. The sin is in knowingly placing appetite before and above consciousness of duty to a higher purpose.

Circumstances or motive can turn a normal appetite into a sinful act. The man who has knowledge that someone is lying at his door starving to death, yet he indifferently sits down to eat his moderate daily meal, that man is indulging his appetite wickedly. Though he would be fulfilling a God-given drive for food, the indulgence of his appetite would be rendered sinful by his knowledge of the hungry man dying outside his door.

A person who, for whatever reason, is persuaded that he should not eat, yet surrenders his convictions to his passions, has committed the same transgression as Eve—allowing bodily appetite to rule the soul.

Ambition

This half-truth, that they would *"be like the gods, knowing good and evil,"* could be an effective temptation only because of the natural seed of ambition that was part of their created human natures. A person can direct his ambition toward righteousness, as do the righteous angels, or toward evil, as did Lucifer when he had ambition to *"be like the most high."* Thus, appealing to their ambition, the tempter led them to think how eating of the tree could advance their station in life, broaden their horizons, elevate them into a higher order of beings—they would *"be like the gods."*

In regulating their exposure to the knowledge of good and evil, God was not trying to keep Adam and Eve from something that was inherently evil, for He Himself was wise, possessing knowledge of good and evil—as He revealed when He said, *"They are become as one of us, knowing good and evil."*

All cultures have their "holy men," seers, prophets, philosophers, monks, gurus—men who give themselves wholly to the task of seeking out the "secrets of the universe." They seek "illumination." They delve into the "hidden," the divinely concealed. "To know" is their goal. This search goes beyond science. It is a journey within as well as a journey to the outer limits. "To be like the gods" is the highest state of being. The thing that makes such a quest evil is that, just as Eve, this knowledge is sought for personal elevation and advancement. It promises power! One neglects his humanity for a chance at deity. Those who reach the higher plane, their nirvana, would rather associate with the spirits, be they good or evil, than to resume their duties among mortals. The pride they feel as a result of this "enlightenment" often puts them beyond religious repentance. Being in touch with the gods, they have become unteachable where it concerns mere mortals.

The evil was not in what they did, nor in what they came to know, but in their faithless, independent rebellion against the clear word of their Creator. Their fall was more than a fall from paradise. It was a fall from mutual confidence and respect. It was a breach of trust. They disdained friendship with God.

The root

Furthermore, none of the drives that provided occasions for them to be tempted (nor the drives that provide occasions for us to be tempted today) was innately evil.

The root of all sin is found in the runaway indulgence of God-given desires. A shoplifter is drawn to steal through the sight of his eyes. An adulterer is draw away by lust originating in natural bodily desires.

Satan did not—and can not—create a single passion in man. He can only steer us to use our God-given drives and abilities in a selfish way. Through association and misuse, he can then twist our appetites to become channels for satanic compulsions. He commandeers godly impulses and produces runaway indulgence.

Beasts of the earth do not have the capacity to make moral decisions, denying natural drives. They are within their intended bounds living for self-gratification. But a person who puts aside his higher intellect and conscience to subsist on passions of the body has degenerated to the rudiments of a dumb animal.

Our drives are like the gas pedal on an automobile; there is no governor to limit the speed. Passions were not intended to be indiscriminately accelerated. They have no built-in discretion, but God gave us intelligence with which to regulate the indulgence of our passions.

Understand, the couple's goal was not to break fellowship with God or to attempt to overthrow His kingdom. They did not desire to switch sides and join a rebellion. They did not desire to be evil. They certainly did not want to die. Then wherein was their sin?

This first temptation was not a lusty passion to do the diabolical or the lascivious; it was a temptation to break out of the discipline place upon them, to press their capacities to the limit without regard to personal trust or mutual respect. Eve following the flesh, and Adam, for reasons of his own, broke free from the confinement of a relationship with God.

The first couple

God gave Adam and Eve the power to choose and then provided the menu: the Tree of Life, lovingly provided by the Father to sustain life, or the tree that would give sudden knowledge of good and evil. They could choose the sweet fruit of trust and obedience or the bitter fruit of self-will and regret.

They stood innocent, well informed, and suitably warned. It was an issue of trust, believing God to provide all that is needful or of doubting His good intentions and reaching for all they could get. They chose the shortcut of gratification and immediate enlightenment.

Lest He violate the integrity of their personhood, God could not invade their wills to prevent them from exercising choice. Yet He grieved as they betrayed His trust and hid from His fellowship. They stood crossways to God's purposes in the universe, but He could not annihilate them; they were made alive with His eternal spirit.

Eve doubted God's good intentions. She did not believe God, and *"without faith it is impossible to please Him."* Faith in one's friend is no arbitrary condition to fellowship. It is a deep wound to have a friend doubt your good intentions. To doubt the sincerity or truthfulness of someone is to slight their character. By gratifying her senses and rushing into a knowledge of good and evil, Eve disregarded God. It was an act of unfaithfulness. It was spiritual adultery.

When they used their freedom to experience selfish gratification the strings were cut and the drift began. With the help of an advisor, Lucifer, they had conceived human sin. God had placed them on a road that went in two directions. He stood at one end and advised them to come toward Him, warning them of death if they went the other way. Eve was deceived through her drives and the lies of the Tempter; but Adam, not at all deceived, chose to turn his back on God and follow his new bride into the false promises of independence.

Failure?

It would seem that God had attempted an experiment that ended in failure. Did He allow too much independence, too much creativity and originality? Should He have limited His creations to peacocks and colored carp in an aquatic paradise?

Adam took the power to choose and ran in the wrong direction. Free will, with no strings attached, proved to be a costly gift. God sought a family and ended up with contenders for preeminence.

Inventors

Future generations followed in Adam's moral footsteps, demonstrating rebellious individuality and ingenuity. They designed ever-new ways to over-indulge and abuse their bodies. But God did not step in and remove their liberty. He continued to respect their personhood and did not bully them into submission. Some mistook His silence as approval. Others claimed that no such God above themselves ever existed. Eventually an alternative had to be found to explain man's origins. It came to be called *evolution*.

Man's attempt to build community without God came to be called *culture*. His attempt to explain the selfish motivations of the human heart came to be called *psychology*. Various endeavors to appease the offended deities and satiate the conscience came to be called *religion*—and later, *philosophy*. The record of man's inhumanity to man and his rejection of God is called *history*.

Chapter Four
Things God Cannot Do.

The question is asked:

"Could not God have created a race of beings who were incapable of sin?" We answer: No, God cannot create persons constitutionally unable to sin. To exclude all possibility of sin, it would have been necessary for God to have permitted no freedom of will higher than that of animals. To achieve the desired end—persons—God must have allowed free and ungoverned will, which by its very nature admits to the possibility of sin. It was not necessary for God to make persons, but if He would make persons He was limited to those three essential attributes of personhood wherein the will is indispensable.

God limited?

It may shock your sensibilities to think in terms of God being limited (Psalm 78:41). However, this is not a limitation in the normal sense of the word. The manner in which God is limited is actually freedom. The Creator is limited to those means that are consistent with His end—in this case, the end being to make persons. For example, a mathematician who would solve an equation is self-limited to those means that provide the right answer. A logician is limited to the rational. A witness is limited to the truth. A lover is limited to love. He has the freedom not to be a lover, but if he would be a lover he does not have the freedom not to love. A historian is limited to the facts. He may write fiction if he chooses, but if he would write history he is limited to the facts.

Likewise, there are some things God cannot do, not for lack of power but for want of conformity to His own nature and purposes. He has the constitutional power to do any and all conceivable alternatives, but His wisdom renders many options impossible. BY CHOICE, God cannot do the irrational, the arbitrary, or the unjust.

Moral Nature

Truth did not gain eminence over falsehood simply because God decided it would. Truth was not arbitrarily elected as the standard. Truth can never be a lie, nor can a lie be the truth. The intrinsic goodness and desirability of truth does not emanate from God's choice, but from His nature. God is truth. Life is not a game with rules that could have been different from what they are. God's moral nature is the moral nature of all He created.

Therefore, we can be sure that the concepts by which we judge right and wrong are not arbitrary. That is, the case is not such that if God were to do the preposterous, declaring evil to be good and good to be evil, such a declaration would not make it so. We have an inherent sense of right and wrong that is a reflection of God's nature, the prototype of our own. The same principles of right and wrong exist in all moral beings, including God. It could not be otherwise. God is truth, love, justice, logic, intelligence, independent will, etc., so the same becomes the measure by which all things are constituted.

Physical Nature

The same harmony and consistency is evident in the physical realm. The laws inherent within the entire physical and metaphysical world are after the nature of God. This is both rational and desirable. The alternative would be chaos. For example, mathematics is not something arbitrarily created that could have existed under different rules. The harmony and intrinsic logic of math is a reflection of the nature of God and of the inherent order of His creation.

Thus, God is ~~predictable~~ faithful. He will always operate consistent with the rules emanating from His own nature. By eternal choice, God cannot function outside that which is intrinsically intelligent, wise, right, and good.

Human Nature

We are comfortable saying, "God can do anything; surely if he wanted to, He could create a man who couldn't sin." But only chaos is without limitation. It has no order and can therefore entertain contradicting occurrences. Unless God's nature has no constancy, no order – in essence no nature – then He is limited to His own nature. Certainly God has the freedom to choose, but freedom does not imply heedless actions, actions contrary to the inherent order. God's power to choose is unlimited, but his choices are limited by His wisdom.

Therefore, if we humans find fault with God for giving us this unruly nature, or if we regard our freedom as a burden of responsibility for which we do not want to be held accountable, and we blame God for having created humanity so vulnerable, then we are assuming that the Creator chose an unnecessary course. If we propose that God should have created persons without complete freedom of choice, then we are proposing something that is in conflict with the nature of reality (reality emanating from His nature, the fountain of all reality).

To imagine a person who could not think independently or act independently is not to image a person at all; it is to imagine the impossible, the absurd. When our definition of a person takes us outside the essential attributes of personhood, it has taken us to a land of dreams and wishful thinking, into chaos where anything can exist with no consequences—and ultimately, no meaning.

God's nature, the pattern

Therefore, having decided to make persons like Himself, persons with whom He could fellowship, God was limited to His own nature as the pattern. God cannot make a person who is less than a person, so all the necessary attributes of personhood must be incorporated into the persons God would make. If a being is to relate to God, he must be in God's image. If a person is in Gods image, he will necessarily possess attributes of soul like God's soul (though obviously not on an infinite level). Since freedom of the will is an essential part of being a person, God could not make a person who was not free to choose. His nature entails free will, and therefore a person in His image must have free will. A person who was not endowed with the constitutional option to choose between sin and righteousness would be without will and thus without personhood.

Questions on free will:

The question is asked: "Could not God have given them a free will in everything except where it applied to sin?" If God had given them a will, but then kept some invisible strings attached or placed some internal governor, rendering their wills inoperative when they were in danger of sinning, then they would not have been humans, just puppets. We would say that personhood is diminished in proportion to the diminishing of free will, but actually any erosion of freewill is a complete elimination of personhood. Unless individuality (autonomous personhood) is a farce, God could never interfere with the constitutional function of the human will. Even a stray cat chooses its master.

Full Dimension

As we have amply shown, just as all three dimensions are necessary to maintain the very concept of space, so mind, emotions, and will are all necessary to maintain the concept of humanity. There are essential elements in the nature of a thing that cannot be diminished in the least without completely altering its nature. To remove one dimension does not diminish space by one-third; it destroys the very concept of space. God cannot make space that is only two-dimensional. Such would be contrary to the reality of His own likeness, and therefore the likeness of all things. The human soul, existing in God's likeness, is triune. If one element is missing, the image of God is removed, and that which remains is by nature no longer a person. As conscious thought is essential to the concept of mind, likewise free choice is essential to the concept of human will. Personhood is indivisible. To cause the will to be dysfunctional or to diminish it in the least would be to lose the image of God—to lose human nature. It would be a cessation of one of the three essential attributes of personhood, and thus of personhood itself.

The question is asked:

"Why could not God have given them a free will, but then stopped them from sinning?" God's capacity for brute overriding force does not make the exercise of it desirable. We tend to think of power alone as the ultimate reality. To God, truth, love, and righteousness are before power. A governor once wrote out a pardon to a condemned criminal. The criminal refused to sign the pardon. The governor had the power to deny execution but not the moral or legal right. With the pardon still offered right up until the last minute, the condemned man was executed on schedule. Might is not always right. God functions rationally, justly, and according to the law of His nature, which is the law of our nature and the law of the universe.

A parent may grieve at the attitude of his child. The child may be small enough and the parent strong enough to forcibly prevent any action, but the parent understands that it is counterproductive to violate the child's freedom to choose. The parent would like to invade the child's inner soul and change his will, but it is impossible to do so. Not even God has rightful access to the sacred seat of the individual's soul. To forcibly invade the "command and control room" of the soul would constitute Divine rape. To do so would destroy human personality. Having created us in His own image, God respects our individual autonomy. God's only recourse is that of persuasion. He who will not be persuaded exercises his God-endowed right to stand in defiance of the highest wisdom, goodness, and law. God never walks through the door of another person unless invited in. He never detains a man to listen unless the man pauses and lends his ear.

The question is asked:

"Why could not God have given them a free will and permitted them to exercise it, but just not allowed any opportunity to sin, like not putting the tree in the garden?"

The presence of the tree did not create a foreign opportunity to sin. Sin does not come from outside us, as from the thing that lures our appetites. It comes from the decided selfish use of our human attributes. The presence of appetite and passion eventually would have led to a moral challenge. Through the presence of the tree, God actually made it easier on them by making the moral challenge objective. The challenge was external, so well defined that Eve was able to verbally define the issues to her tempter.

without God you would have 2D, second rate, we would get very frustrated and annoyed. Nothing would work. Argh Hell.

Question:

"But sin is evil. Why must the possibility of evil be a part of God's nature and therefore a part of ours?" The point we have well established is that human nature is designed after the pattern of God's nature, and of necessity must have the two-way moral capacity. The tree of knowledge was knowledge of opposites, *good and evil.* When God created a man who could give love, He was also creating a man who could withhold that love. Freedom is multidirectional. Lurking just in the shadows of every good opportunity is its evil counterpart. If you abolished the concept of the negative, the positive would disappear with it. God can be good without the presence of sin, but he could not be known to be good by one who did not have knowledge of evil.

As we have seen, righteousness can only come from a free moral agent. Learning cannot exist where ignorance is not possible. Giving is not possible where selfish possession is not possible. To give, one must have the power to retain. For a person's benevolence to be meaningful, self-centeredness must be possible. God cannot create a mouth capable of blessing except it be equally capable of cursing. When God created light, He made shadows a possibility. Darkness is indefinable apart from light. Love is only possible where hate is also possible. To be loved has meaning only where it is freely and voluntarily given.

Moral capacity is a two-way street. You cannot make a street that physically goes only one way. A man walking down a street in one direction is thereby conscious of the opposing direction. You cannot have an *up* without having a *down.* You cannot have an *in* without having an *out.* You cannot have a magnetic field without a positive and a negative. There can be no time without a past, present, and future. There can be no person in the image of God without mind, emotion, and will. There can be no will except it is free to choose. If God would create a man at all, the man must be capable of responsible choice. To possess the capacity to choose is to admit to the possibility of choosing selfishly. The men God would create must be capable of sinning, for the capacity for sinning comes with the capacity for righteousness.

Artists can choose their mediums and subjects, and musicians can choose their melodies. Statesmen can shape their kingdoms, and men can become slave owners or missionaries. Where men and women can sell their vegetables, they can also sell their bodies. In a world where one can use his strength to assist another, he can also use his strength to make war against another. Where truth can be printed, a lie can become headlines. A man capable of putting his trust in God is also capable of trusting only himself.

I hear someone challenging: "If the *image and likeness* of God necessarily entails a will capable of sinning, are you saying that God can sin?" God has the innate capacity to do anything that He pleases. He is not prevented from free exercise of His will by some law higher than Himself. If God chose to act contrary to His own eternal character, if He chose to do the preposterous and act against Himself and His own righteous purposes, He has the capacity to do so. But, due to His attribute of omniscience (knowing all), God *"cannot be tempted with evil."* Perfect knowledge of all events, past, present and future, would prevent Him from ever being deceived or making a mistake in judgment. Complete knowledge coupled with perfect wisdom and goodness makes it certain God would never choose to sin. His righteous choices do not come from naive innocence, but from holy character supported by infinite knowledge. God is free to choose and freely chooses to do only good. It is His desire that we be equally free and equally committed to holy choice.

Question:

"If one day Christians are going to be sinless in heaven, why could not God have created us with just such a holy nature?"

Righteousness is not an attribute of nature. It cannot be created. It is an attribute of soul. It is metaphysical—beyond nature. Nature is that which is governed by fixed laws. It is impersonal, whereas moral goodness and badness assumes intelligence. Duty to be righteous is the innate responsibility of all self-conscious beings. Nothing in physical nature can contemplate values and be aware of duty. To speak of being by-nature righteous or evil is confusing the physical and the metaphysical.

Sinning is imperfect

God cannot create character. The very nature of character necessitates it be achieved only through experience. We know this to be true both by reason and by revelation. Adam and Eve, as well as Lucifer and the Angels, were innocent from their inception, but they obviously had no character. Reason tells us that character is vitally linked to experience. Only by facing morally opposing options, weighing the value of each, and then following through with a choice do we develop character. God could not do the nonsensical and create a man with immediate character. Character cannot be inherited. Your child was not born with your character. Character is personal and individual. Positive character is the possession of those who have developed a value system and then endured the test of temptation.

God desires to have mature sons and daughters who possess solid, dependable character. Confirmed character is molded in the struggles between good and evil. One must see the end of evil and compare it with the good in order to develop a permanent preference for the good. Character becomes stronger with every resisted temptation. No doubt, the righteous angels were further confirmed in their righteousness when Lucifer demonstrated the consequences of his own sin.

If God would have men of character, He must permit them free and unhindered self-determination. It cannot be a mock battle. If they would learn to walk they must be permitted to fall. Parents can give birth to their children and train them to make moral decisions, but there comes a time when parental control is limited. No child ever learned to ride a bicycle with his parents holding the handlebars. Eventually parents must turn loose of little hands and allow them to face moral decisions alone. God has allowed each of us to go it alone. He endowed us with a freedom that extends to the ability to use it against Him.

So, it was an either-or situation: to create nothing higher than a chimpanzee, or create a being like Himself who could have the freedom of self-determination. There was no risk in the former, but neither was there any potential.

God cannot make a man with inherent knowledge of good and evil. That knowledge comes only with the exercise of the will in regard to moral choices. A man must choose between good and evil if he is to know either. Regardless of the choice, whether one chooses good or chooses evil, just the exercise of making a value judgment brings about an understanding of good and evil. If Adam and Eve had said "No" to the temptation, they would have experienced a brief glimpse into the moral realm (good and evil). With each successive victory they would have grown in righteousness. Every time they said "No" to the tree they would have been more confirmed in righteousness. It would have resulted in the development of character. They would have known evil from afar, while they would have known righteousness intimately.

The Creator endowed us with great potential. That which God desired in us but could not create was potentially present in Adam's nature. As we have seen, only through individual free choice is godly character possible.

Values are formed by evaluating alternatives and weighing their moral worth. Our character springs from the values we have assumed. The history of our faithfulness to those values demonstrates our character. To create a man with innate character would be to create him with a past history, a stored-up memory of value judgments. Man could not be created like God, with an eternal past, but a past is necessary for character. To have character like God, man needed a history. God could not make a man with a pre-installed, fictional history in his consciousness. A newly created man with a memory of the past would be deceived. God would be causing him to believe fiction as history. What he took to be his past experience in reality would be God's fictional account. It would be confusion, playing games, a suspension of the nature of truth—a lie. The man would be a farce, a fantasy creation. That which is inconsistent with the nature of reality is inconsistent with the nature of God and therefore impossible.

Moral workshop

The ongoing history of man is not an accident in progress. It is a moral workshop. Life is a character clinic. It is a principles factory, a boot camp of trials and testings designed to improve our moral fiber. The obstacles are not part of an unfinished playground; they are designed for maximum training of the "students." For the purpose of moral development, God placed us in this fragile state of need and dependence.

Whoever would have God do the impossible, creating a fairy-tale kingdom of perfectly submissive, intelligent, and loving individuals with no struggle and no triumph, would write a novel that began with "And they lived happily ever after." What were they happy about? What sense of accomplishments did they possess? Were there any heroes? Did they sing melancholy songs of lost opportunity and joyous songs of love won, or did they sing at all? Did they have any pride or shame? Were they thankful? To whom and for what? Did they learn anything? Did they grow?

God could have created a race of potted plants, but instead He created gardeners endowed with the freedom to grow vegetables or marijuana.

A *Being* in God's image can think an original thought. He can do a creative original deed. He holds the reins to his own buggy. He takes the keys and goes out in the car by himself. He decides where he will go. He flies solo. He is indeed the master of his ship, the captain of his "unconquerable soul." He can chart his course by God's stars or he can get drunk and sleep at the wheel. He can bless God or curse the day he was born. This a man can do with absolute confidence, knowing his Creator will never commandeer his soul.

God can rebuke a storm at sea and it immediately calms. He can reshape the earth or the heavens by His word alone, but He will not be a bully and take captive the will of another. He will not commit piracy and seize the piloting of your soul. Your soul is your sacred ground. You can mold it after the image of the lovely and pure, or you can drag it into the sewer of filthy flesh.

The imagination can take God's magic wand and create a make-believe world that is without risk, danger, or loss. But real humanity cries out for the freedom to break loose and run with the winds of change and growth. We would limit God to the painting of perfect clouds in an unchanging sky. Yet for wise reasons that are filled with life, He tossed His clouds up and let the winds carry them over the horizon. Glory comes to the overcomer through contest and triumph, not through the routine of the fixed and limited.

The ultimate state of sinlessness will not be based on wills incapable of evil choice, rather, upon hearts set steadfastly upon righteous choice. The thing that will give continuing glory to God with every passing day of eternity is that each soul continues in God's presence by choice alone.

A summary

Ants communicate with ants. Dolphins communicate with dolphins. But ants and dolphins cannot communicate with each other. Likewise, neither God nor man can fellowship with the lower animal and insect kingdoms. We were designed in God's own image that we might live in fellowship with Him. God's personhood, including free unrestrained will, must be reproduced (albeit on a much smaller scale) if He would create family members, brothers, sisters, children, and friends.

God could have created us as robots, maintaining programmed control, but He would never have felt loved. He would have been bored with our "obedience." If God had been content to surround Himself with palace animals and mechanical "people," He could have maintained a universe that was always in perfect harmony with His will. There would never have been anyone to question His purposes, never any conflict of wills or interests. Only individuals endowed with a free functioning will can discuss a subject and agree or disagree. With no discussions, there would have been no arguments and no hurt feelings.

Sub-humans don't have ambition. Without ambition, there would have been no avarice or stealing. Without intellect, there would have been no skeptics. Without passion, there would have been no lusts. Without emotion, there would have been no hate—or love. Without the mind, there would have been no cunning and no fraud, nor would there have been any benevolence. Without free will there could have been no rebellion and no disobedience. Furthermore, without our limited knowledge and need there could have been no faith. God could have remained in a peaceful, no-risk state if He had chosen to create only physical nature and animals. But He took the present course, knowing the end result would be worth the cost in human and Divine suffering.

Chapter Five
Opposition by Design

Obstacles

In Molding our environment so as to make it morally and physically challenging our Creator has deemed it appropriate to expose the human race to three impediments to goodness of character: the world, the flesh, and the Devil. While being contrary to goodness, they actually provide the necessary struggles on which positive character is built.

The World—Vanities of Vanities

This very planet is under a curse by God. It does not yield its agricultural increase as originally intended. It is a struggle just to survive the elements. We have a very narrow comfort zone. When it is 65 we are cold. When it is 80 we are hot. Different from the animals, our bodies are not equipped for survival. Without clothes and shelter we are as vulnerable as a displaced baby rabbit that doesn't yet have its fur.

The *world* itself is not evil, but it provides the ingredients for the satiating of any lust. It is the counterpart to the flesh. All that the flesh can desire is readily sold in the world's bazaar. It hocks its wares to the innocent, often providing the first forbidden dose free of charge. It then peddles its fare to the mature connoisseurs of pleasure, never revealing the awful price. We have fallen in love with the world and bought stocks in its futures. To us the world has become more than a planet; it is a mistress promising secret indulgences.

Our societies have become dumps for moral hazardous wastes. In the past, social and moral corruption began in the seaports and oozed its way inland, finding fertile ground in the largest cities. After breeding there, like fleas on a dog it hitchhiked its way into the rural areas. But today moral plagues have a more rapid form of transmission. Television, radio, and the internet instantly and intravenously feed Hollywood junkies with the latest corruption. The addicts rush home from work to get their fix. Earthlings are constantly bombarded with propaganda that is designed to feed lust, pride, and rebellion. One who knows said, *"Love not the world, neither the things that are in the world. If any man love the world, the love of the Father is not in him. For the world passeth away and the lust thereof, but he that doeth the will of the Father abideth forever (1 John 2:15)."*

The Flesh — *Body of Corruption*
The second obstacle to goodness is the flesh. When God linked the human soul to a body of flesh it was like confining the wind to a hollow tree. The substance of soul and flesh are not only different, they are contrary in nature. This is not to say that the flesh is evil. It is inanimate and therefore has no moral quality. It is neither good nor bad. Yet human flesh is similar to a fungus or a mold—mindlessly it wants to feed, reproduce and live.

Since the human race sinned in Adam the struggles between the flesh and spirit have greatly intensified. The flesh, in its effort to be gratified, struggles to overcome the spirit. Likewise the spirit strives to govern the fleshly animal instincts. Though it is not inevitable that it should be so, the desires of the flesh have taken varying degrees of dominance over the intentions of the human spirit. So the flesh and spirit stand in opposition to each other.

The human body (flesh) did not become mortal as a result of sin. The fleshly body was never meant to be eternal. Prior to their sin, it was necessary for Adam and Eve to eat in order to sustain their mortal bodies. They were given access to *The Tree Of Life,* an indication that their bodies were created mortal. After sinning, they were deprived of access to this life-perpetuating tree, which prevented them from continuing to live forever.

The Scriptures tell us in 1Cor. 15: 38-54 that God gave Adam *"a body as it hath pleased him* [pleased God]," a body that was said to be *"earthy"* instead of *"heavenly,"* *"natural"* instead of *"spiritual,"* a body existing in *"weakness."* But then it was intended to be only a *"seed"* foreshadowing the *"glory"* of a future *"spiritual body"* yet to be realized. This antagonism between the body and soul existed before the fall of Adam and Eve.

This temporary physical body, called *"the flesh,"* and in another place, *"vile body,"* plays a significant role in the development of character. The body, with its carnal needs, provides a ready potential to lust. To compound the natural pull of the flesh, since the fall this *"body of corruption"* is subject to fatigue and disease. When we are in a weakened state it is harder to consider the needs of others and to be caring toward them.

Most of our time here on earth is consumed in the care of this flesh. It is easy to become preoccupied with survival. This earthy flesh has legitimate needs, but we have a tendency to allow pleasure and personal comfort to become primary. We would all be poets and prophets; we would let our spirits soar, but our flesh drags us to the table, the toilet, the dentist, the doctor, and the grave.

The body affords endless opportunity for various indulgences, whereby many find solace in the corporate drowning of their consciences in the pool of self-gratification. Enslavement to gratification and preoccupation with ambition has left us with feelings of moral helplessness.

By nature the flesh is neither good nor evil. Being an inanimate conglomerate of biological tissue, it can have no moral quality. However, if the soul living in the body gives itself over to exist for bodily satisfaction, the body becomes filled with inordinate lusts. It is then a *flesh full of sin*—in the Bible called: *"sinful flesh."* The flesh is not sinful by nature. It is sinful by application. And we are the applicators.

As each of us in turn has proven, the flesh is a powerful persuader. Natural lusts of the flesh exert an awful pull, but the flesh can be further conditioned to entertain ever new and bizarre lusts. Normal appetites, when inordinately indulged, can compound into unnatural passions. These dark passions are mutations of human invention that metastasize into monstrous consuming lusts, possessing the soul like a thousand demons. The flesh then takes on a form and likeness that is more comparable to a creation of Satan than to the image of God. As God created it, the flesh is a testing ground. But after we have fed it an inordinate diet of forbidden fare, it becomes a dark prison house of mutated monsters, fit only for the worms of Hell.

God did not create us in an imposition. The inner man, the soul and spirit, is indeed capable of exercising authority over this flesh. As we saw earlier, the purpose of linking soul to body is to provide the kind of struggles the soul needs in order to grow. If one did overcome this body of corruption, indeed he would be a champion of righteousness.

Lucifer

The third impediment to our efforts at goodness comes from one who does not want us to trust our Creator. He is the master deceiver; the father of all lies. He is leading a universal rebellion against the Divine Kingdom. He is the champion of sinful flesh, the purveyor of all filth and doubt. Satan plays a key role in our testing. He spends his time thinking of new and deceitful ways to trick us into selfish indulgence. Those who overcome him will have endured every possible evil scenario. Eternity future will not be able to turn up any new temptations. Those who overcome here will overcome anywhere.

Satan seeks the ruin of God's program. His main sphere of activity is not the Mafia, but religion. He craves worship. First, he likes to be highly regarded. Second, he wants to be feared. He has millions of disembodied evil spirits in his service. Since they have lost their bodies, they seek gratification through those humans who still have flesh. They cannot force anyone to indulge, but they will surely reinforce one's decision to do so. Only rarely do we confront these evil spirits in a tangible way. They are damned and seek the same for everyone. The Apostle said, *"We wrestle not against flesh and blood, but against principalities, against powers, against the rulers of the darkness of this world, against spiritual wickedness in high places (Eph. 6:12)."*

Satan would see us become inhuman. In contrast, God seeks our freedom and values our individuality, making humanity a step up into divine sonship. Satan would use humanity as a step down into the animal, the carnal, the base, the ugly, and the defiled. He delights to see God deprived of our fellowship, to see us subsist on appetite and passion rather than intellect. It he can direct our natural passions sufficiently to make us addicts to perversion, he knows we will become consumers of a product that only he can supply. Our carnal union to him as benefactor of the flesh is a love/hate relationship, but one in which he gets satisfaction from a twisted kind of worship. Where God created us finite with a destiny in the infinite, Satan would see our finite souls shrivel until they are cannibalized by our own lusts. Satan would turn us inward where there is no thought and no imagination except in the indulgence of appetite. Through subversion he would destroy music, art, language, design, dignity, natural sexuality, any form of creativity and positive expression. He conceals himself and feeds us in anticipation of the day when depression causes us to despair of any destiny greater than consumption. His entanglements are first gentle and subtle, but with addiction his laughter is soon heard above our empty prayers.

In contrast, God desires free association. He would see us grow, mature, become like Himself. He desires our individuality, not our consumption. God would expand himself, not by consuming our personalities but by our voluntarily sharing His.

However, the presence of the Tempter is not an unfortunate obstacle. To those in submission to God's program, he is a moral hurdle that builds spiritual muscle. As a contender for the crown he provides opportunity for us to overcome. Without a challenger there could be no overcomers, no champions, and no glory.

The plan

Those who overcome Planet Earth, the body of corruption, and the Prince of Darkness will have developed into persons far beyond anyone God could have directly created. Conditions could not be more suitable to the development of character than they are in this present environment. We are not surviving a misfortune or rebuilding from an accident; we are developing in an environment perfectly suited to the end God has in view. The fall of Adam (of the human race) was not necessary, but neither is it a misfortune from which God is trying to recover. God is working all things *to the praise and glory of His grace.* A sovereignty that would permit free will would do so with foreknowledge of the consequences, and would therefore only commence a history that would end consistent with His own values and goals.

Making a king's son

A long time ago in a faraway land, an aging, benevolent king contemplated the successor to his throne. The sons of his youth were well provided. They enjoyed the show and the pomp but most of all they loved the power. Being of the royal class they never needed to work. Their hands were not callused and their bodies bore no scars. None of them could tell you what it felt like to be hungry or poor. They were fit to be neither kings nor men. The king could trust none of them with his kingdom.

Unknown to the public or his other sons, the king took the son of his old age and placed him in a peasant family. The child was too young to understand his origin. The king's instructions were that the child was to receive no special treatment. He was to labor, be poor, suffer deprivation, and be hungry in his turn.

As he grew to be a young man, he came to understand more of who he was, but he did not know exactly what that might entail. He never felt special, and he didn't know that his life was actually a school to prepare him for the throne. In poverty he labored, sometimes to despair.

He occasionally heard the stories of his origin but he doubted them. He reasoned that if he were really the king's son he would not struggle and suffer. When at last he became convinced that he was indeed of royal blood he doubted his father's good will toward him.

The day came when he was called to the palace where he was received as heir to the throne. On that day he discovered that his father the King had indeed continually monitored his progress and even arranged circumstances to enhance his education and character building. The rough circumstances of peasantry had made him the kind of man the king desired to sit on the throne. The young man became a wise and compassionate king. He could identify with his subjects and was of such character that he did not give-in to the vanity and pride of his office.

What the King could not do in a protected environment, he had accomplished in the trials of independent struggle. God cannot *create* worthy sons. They are forged in the furnace of trials and moral challenges.

Seedlings

In late winter we plant our garden seeds in small pots and allow them to germinate indoors where they can be protected. As it gets a little warmer and the plants larger, we place them outdoors in a protected bed. They are covered for warmth and provided with artificial heat at night. On days when it is 40 degrees outside the sun will shine through the plastic covering and the plants will be in an 80-degree, humid environment. The plants grow as in the Garden of Eden.

For years my neighbors have been making their living selling produce. During my first year as a would-be farmer I tried to follow their example, giving my plants extra attention, making sure they were always warm and well watered. I would go by my neighbors' houses and notice they didn't take advantage of some of the bright sunny days. My plants would be covered and growing profusely in an 80 or 90-degree environment while their plants would be uncovered, getting knocked around by a 50-degree breeze. My plants very quickly outgrew theirs, becoming taller and greener. When it came time to plant outdoors, my plants were twice as tall as theirs. However, after being in the ground for a week, many of my carefully nurtured plants had died. The others struggled for survival until they eventually fell behind my neighbors' smaller plants.

I made inquiries and discovered that they had deliberately exposed their plants to harsh conditions so they would toughen up to survive in their future environment. Their plants became acclimated to the harshness of real life. They had exposed their plants to hardship in a controlled way. They did not always keep them well watered. The cold made them grow thick stems and stubby, resistant leaves. The harsh environment prepared them for their sojourn in the garden. I learned my lesson. I now do likewise.

My point is clear. The environment God prepared for us is not intended to be ideal for these bodies of flesh. It is not our bodies God seeks to strengthen, but our souls. Our bodies are a part of the challenging environment. Overcomers will come forth as plantings for the Divine garden.

All of mankind is enrolled in the universal workshop of moral development. Moral standing does not come easily. It demands that we deny immediate gratification and assume responsibility for all our choices.

Chapter Six
Unwilling Sinners?

Victims of the Divine plan?

It is a commonly held belief that our whole life is mapped out before we are born. It is not unusual to hear some inmates in the state prison system express how they are just fulfilling God's great plan for their lives. A few of them reason that if a sovereign God knows everything before it happens, then nothing in life could have been different; we are confined to the Divine plan; all our steps are pre-planned and unalterable. If you find yourself in prison for committing a crime, remember, you are just fulfilling your destiny; you can't help what you are.

When men who reason thus are turned back out on the streets they are not going to take responsibility to alter a life they see as predestinated.

Likewise, Christians have imposed a responsibility upon God that He never assumed. We tie strings to our finances, our children, our car, our health, etc. and then shove the other end up toward heaven. "Now God, you can't let anything bad happen to me or mine; after all, you are sovereign." Then when something of ours gets broken and we find the strings unattended, lying atop the wreckage, we accuse, "Why, God?" Violated spiritual laws have their consequences just as violated physical laws. We are all subject to the law of sowing and reaping.

Design Flawed? How many times have we heard someone glibly dismissing his responsibility for sin? "Well it's just my sinful nature, after all, nobody is perfect." Such morally suicidal beliefs are even supported by some theologies. There are those who hold as cardinal doctrine that, though originally created with a free will, when Adam sinned the human race lost its power to make positive moral choices. Where men feel that sin is an inevitable result of a birth flaw they will never accept responsibility for it. To plead inability based on enslavement of will is the most common excuse of saint and sinner alike. As we have seen, a will that is limited to only evil is no longer making a choice and therefore no longer a will.

If the will has become inoperative then the whole concept of accountability is destroyed. Blame would be unknown. If Hitler did not have a free will, he was not responsible for his actions. Is a drunk free not to drink and drive? Is he to blame? Was there a point at which he could have chosen not to start drinking, or was he born without ability to say no to alcohol? What about drug pushers or child molesters? Should they be treated as if they had no choice?

Many sermons are preached and great volumes are written seeking to disprove the obvious function of free will. To attempt to persuade me to deny my own free will is to call upon me to exercise that which I am not supposed to have. If I have no free will, how could I be persuaded? If you do convince me to change my views, you have caused me to choose, and thus have proven I am capable of free choice. For the proponents of the no free will doctrine to even debate the point is a denial of their position. It is much like inviting people to a lecture where you intend to prove that you do not exist.

In reality, those who deny the attribute of free will do not really believe their own position. In practical ways they continually deny their own doctrine. A man who did not believe in a free will would not be angry with one who burglarized his house—the burglar had no choice in the matter. If your children do not have free wills it is a waste of time to instruct them.

When you are angry toward a man for his degrading or offensive behavior, you are assuming he could have acted differently. To blame is to impute responsibility, to assume free, responsible choice. The man who blames another does indeed believe in free will regardless of his academic claim to the contrary.

Dead will?

When Adam and Eve exercised their God-given wills to disobey God, their wills did not cease to function; neither did they get stuck on disobedience. God did not destroy their capacity to choose. Did the unlawful exercise of God-given human will change the very constitution of the will? To exercise the inherent ability to choose could not possibly destroy the power to choose. Did one wrong choice thereby affirm all future choices to be on the side of evil?

Sinful Abel, the son of sinful Adam, offered an acceptable sacrifice to God. He did the right thing the right way for the right reason. Was he defying a will that was fixed on doing only evil?

Man is universally conscious of his duty and his ability to do the right thing. If we cannot choose to do good, how is it that we know what good is? How is it that we expect it of others? Why do we feel guilt when we fail? Why do we blame ourselves for not being good? Are we that irrational?

We suffer guilt only when we know we have acted differently from how we should have acted. No one feels an obligation to act in a manner he deems impossible. Guilt, being self-incrimination, only occurs when we blame ourselves for our failure. So the universality of guilt is irrefutable testimony to the universal belief that we are indeed capable of willing to do good.

The problem is not in the function of the human will, as seen by the fact that not everyone is overcome of temptation. And those who are overcome are not overcome all the time; and those who are overcome all the time in one area are not overcome in all areas. Furthermore, when a man makes an attempt to do good, even if it is a failed attempt, he has demonstrated his willingness and has expressed his confidence that he is indeed capable of doing his intentions.

There is no such thing as a will that is not free. It is nonsense, a contradiction of terms. To prefix the word *will* with the word *free* is a redundancy. The very concept of a will supposes free and unhindered choice. To speak of a will that is not free is like speaking of a mountain that has no elevation or of an ocean that has no water. Entering into dialogue on whether or not we retain a free will makes us feel as foolish as the man screaming that he had lost his voice.

Convenient excuse: The excuse that our wills are captive comes from our unwillingness to admit being at fault in our sin. We must create an excuse, and it is convenient to interpret our failed moral struggles as a dysfunction of the will itself. We imagine our wills to be dysfunctional because we know that if such were true it would be a perfect alibi. To charge a man's evil to the faulty constitution of his soul is to acquit him of all blame. Who then would be to blame but the creator of this captive will?

"To will is present with me."

It is asked, "If the will is not impaired, how is it that men are conscious of willing to do right yet feel compelled to follow their passions?" This was the case with Paul in Romans chapter seven. Attempting to obey the law, yet living in perpetual defeat, he cried out in remorse, *"For what I would, that do I not.... for to will is present with me..."* Observe that if one truly had no will to do good, he would not say, *"will is present with me."* Nor could he characterize himself as doing what he did not want to do. If he wanted to do it, he was willing.

"...but how to perform that which is good I find not.... It is no longer I that do it but sin that dwelleth in me...." *"For I know that in me (that is, in my flesh) dwelleth no good thing:"* The enemy of right doing was not his will, but his *"flesh,"* also called: *"the body of sin, members, body of death, mortal body,"* and *"deeds of the body (Rom. 7-8)."*

O wretched man that I am! who shall deliver me from the body of this death (Rom. 7)?" The human body of flesh is weak and is subject even to uninvited cravings to indulge. When the mind yields to the body and becomes fixed on gratifying it, it is then a *"carnal mind,"* not subject to the law of God (Romans 8:1).

In Galatians 5:17, Paul said, *"For the flesh lusteth against the Spirit, and the Spirit against the flesh: and these are contrary the one to the other: so that ye cannot do the things that ye would."* Note that he possessed the will to obey the law of God. He defines the struggle as between the *flesh* and the *Spirit*.

Concerning the flesh and spirit, Jesus said, *"The spirit indeed is willing, but the flesh is weak (Matt. 26:41)."* Again, the problem was not in the will, but in the weakness of the flesh to comply with the willing spirit.

"For what the law could not do, in that it was weak through the flesh... (Romans 8:3)." Again, the law failed to produce righteousness, not because of a malfunctioned will, but because of the weak, depraved body of flesh.

Paul said: *"But I see another law in my members, warring against the law of my mind, and bringing me into captivity to the law of sin which is in my members (Romans 7:23)."* His mind and will were overcome by the *"law of sin,"* which was *"in his members."* This law of sin was not in his soul, mind, or will, but his members—eyes, ears, hands, feet, sex organs, tongue, etc.

How is it that the flesh usually wins the battle against the will and the spirit? Every flesh addict who is overcome by some carnal vice will occasionally have a time of moral awakening, leading to an attempt to cease his indulgence. Yet he is repeatedly overcome by his passion and returns to his "weakness." Why is this the consistent experience of so many?

The "slave" to sin does not always make his choices based on his reason and values. While desiring to yield to duty and virtue, he may with protest surrender to bodily passions. His "weakness" lies in the fact that he has come to depend on the indulgence so much that he finds it increasingly easier to rationalize his disregard for what he knows is right. Thus, one can *"serve the law of God"* with his *"mind"* while with the flesh he *"serves the law of sin"* (Rom. 7:25).

At those times when indulging causes him discomfort or loss, he may wish that he had a stronger will. But what he imagines to be a stronger will would in fact be a stronger commitment to his own convictions. He may plead that he is helplessly enslaved, but he knows that what he lacks is sufficient motivation to change. His problem is in his moral values. He simply does not value the good enough to deprive his body of the gratification. By his continual, and possibly complete, enslavement he has not demonstrated his constitutional inability to choose good, rather, his lack of moral earnestness.

Passion is not stronger by nature. It is stronger because of what we choose to value. In Romans chapter seven it was a contest in which the *will* lost out to the passions, not a contest in which the *will* was absent. A man whose will is in bondage to indulgence is not a man incapable of choice, but rather a man who has made a series of choices resulting in surrender of his will to his lusts. It should be observed in Romans 7:9 that before Paul reached the state of being in bondage to the *law of sin in his members*, unable to do as he would, he said of himself, *"For I was alive without the law once: but when the commandment came, sin revived, and I died."* His bondage came after a season of yielding to the flesh, while he was still without Christ, living under the law of Moses. We are *"dead in trespasses and sins (Eph. 2:1),"* not dead in the will.

A revived will

Those who claim to have no will to resist often find sudden new strength to do what they previously could not, as was the case with the man who could not stop drinking until he found he would otherwise die in six months. Thereby he was suddenly empowered to overcome his bodily addiction. He made a choice to quit—and did. There is no moral virtue in ceasing to sin for selfish reasons, but it nonetheless demonstrates the reality of a functioning will. When an unregenerate man is conscious of a temptation and, out of a desire to please God, makes a successful choice not to yield, he has confirmed not only the operation but the power of a free will.

Designed flawed?

If enslavement to sin is a constitutional fault in our makeup, if one's will is such that he is incapable of choosing good, he could lay the blame on his Designer. He could say, "I was born this way. Since by nature I cannot choose other than evil, I cannot be blamed." And he would be absolutely correct. He would have the best of all excuses for continuing in sin. Would you find fault with a fish for not swimming upstream to lay its eggs when you had caused it to be confined to a pond? Then how could you intelligently demand that a man act differently from his capabilities? Could God blame us for not doing the impossible?

If sin is an inevitable event emanating from fixed law, are we perpetrators or victims? It is a permissive theology of excuse and indulgence that denies the capacity of free choice.

Depravity

By misusing and abusing the image of God through wrong choices, we have not destroyed our three-fold image; we have criminalized it. On an individual level, in our own personal history of moral choosing, we have become depraved in choice but not depraved in the mechanism of choice—the will itself. To misuse a thing or to use it contrary to its intended purpose is not a depravity of the substance of the thing but a depravity of intent on the part of the abuser. The failure of the will to overcome is not the cause of sin but the result. To speak of human depravity is not to speak of our moral constitution but to speak of our intentions and actions. God is responsible for my attributes (nature); I am responsible for my actions. To blame my actions on my attributes is to excuse myself of responsibility.

We can thus conclude that we are indeed personal souls with free and independently functioning wills. We are responsible to do what we can, accountable to do what we ought, to blame for not doing what we should, and therefore accountable for all lack of conformity to the image of God.

Knowing ourselves in this regard provides a basis for further inquiry.

Chapter Seven
To Blame God

"It's not my fault."

Ah! The newly created mortal rises from the dust, hears the rules read, and then rushes into disobedience. When he is hurt by the experience he then turns to find fault with his Creator. "Why did you give me such liberty?" When the Eternal doesn't answer, he formulates grumbling complaints designed to discredit God's character.

When men's innuendoes and insults do not draw God out into a personal defense, they deny His existence by formulating alternative explanations of their origins. I am reminded of a child, offended at his mother, who responds by denying that he has any mother. In his selfish hurt he seeks to punish her with his denial.

Skeptics, seeking to give credibility to their rejection, attempt to establish intellectual sounding rationale. This drives them to completely irrational positions: denial of a Creator, denial of absolute moral values, denial of absolute truth, denial that we can know anything for sure, denial of the soul as anything more than a temporary allusion of the physical world of nature, etc.

In the name of Philosophy, men will deny the logical conclusions of any discussion, deny the existence of the thing they are denying, then deny their denial. Before they are through, they have denied those very realities that were the bases of their reasoning. I have talked with men who denied their own existence. Meanwhile, they go on indulging the thing that doesn't exist in the things that don't exist. This is the ostrich approach—childhood mentality growing backwards. Their logic is like the man at sea chopping holes in his boat to let the water out, or like the carpenter who couldn't help hitting his thumb, so he solved the problem by denying that it was his thumb.

Eternal goodness—Terminal evil

If men really believe their accusations against God, if they truly think the Creator is not righteous, why do they not create a religion around the concept of an imperfect god? Is it not revealing that the mind of man does not seem to be able to formulate a theology based on belief in a morally imperfect God? We intuitively know that only goodness can be eternal and omnipotent. We accept with unquestioned assurance the assumption that evil is a temporary state of departure, that evil is by nature terminal—self-destructive.

Many primitive peoples are seen appeasing an evil god; but upon closer examination you will find that they believe in a good God who is before or above the evil gods. Universally, all cultures understand life to be a struggle between good and evil, with good being the rightful custodian of the universe. It is only rational to believe in an eternal God of goodness who is the author of the universe.

To believe in self-perpetuating evil is like believing darkness to be the creator of light. It is like believing order is the result of random chaos, or that a sound mind is the product of insanity. Just as heat can become cold, but cold can never become heat, so *good* can degenerate into evil, but evil can never generate into good. Evil is the opposite of creativity, freedom, love, giving. It consumes without giving until there is nothing left but refuse. It devours everything, including itself. We intuitively know that the character of an omnipotent God could be only that of wisdom and love. We sense that if we could locate God we would find Him enthroned in righteousness. To deny this is to deny a most basic universal presupposition.

Nature of the question

We humans have confidently and arrogantly gone our own way until our way has become a tragedy. Then with the excuse that we are seeking answers, through tears and clenched teeth we throw our accusing questions into the darkness where we suspect Deity of concealing Himself.

Why is it that we wait until we are reaping what we have sown before asking those deep theological questions? We pretend to be seeking information, but we are really calling on God to share the blame. "Why did God make a world where there would be suffering? Why did God let all those people die in the earthquake? Why would God make men so they could sin? Why would God send men to hell?" We are not inquiring of God, we are indicting Him—accusing Him of being unworthy of our trust?

When we challenge God thus, we are not expecting an answer; we just want the problem of human suffering to be an unanswerable tragedy, thus relieving us of responsibility. If from the less emotional sidelines someone should give a reasonable answer to life's enigmas we will pretend it is beyond our understanding and continue to scream our questions at the silent God.

He has deferred speaking on His own behalf, not because He is arrogant and delights in our ignorant groveling, but because our questions do not come from sincere inquiry. When a child is told to do something that he doesn't want to do he will demandingly ask, "Why?" The question is not prompted by a spirit of cooperative inquiry but by a spirit of rebellion. The question is cast at the parent as a challenge to his or her wisdom and authority. The child's questions are actually statements of defiance. The wise parent will know that the character of the child is better served if the question is left unanswered. The child should trust the wisdom and good intentions of the parent. In response to criticism God's silence is the loudest statement in the universe.

The issue is not a deficit of information but a deficit of character. The child who is perfectly compliant in spirit doesn't need explanations.

When we question God we are bearing testimony against Him. We have seated ourselves as judges in a courtroom where God is the accused. He is guilty until proven innocent. We withhold our honor and withdraw our submission until He proves Himself judicially worthy. It would be impossible to hold court now and expect God to get a fair trial. The jury is prejudiced by the personal implications of the possibility of exonerating the Creator. To ask the accusers to confess that God is wise and good is asking the condemned to exonerate the judge. Like a zealous prosecuting attorney, we mortals calculatingly frame our questions to entrap God and then turn in triumph to the jury, confident that there is no acceptable answer. Our questions and God's silence are just a part of the record we hope the public will use to convict God of being an unworthy judge. Our subconscious thought is: "With the highest office in scandal who is going to judge me in my transgression?"

Our consciences are quieted by being part of a crowd that mutually distrusts its governor. Personal guilt is dulled and the sense of accountability diminished when we lose ourselves in the masses. Somehow, probably from living under such a permissive philosophy, we think God will find it expedient to withdraw His stern demands.

"He can't damn everybody. Public opinion is against it. The teacher can't fail the whole class; he will have to adjust the curve. Why, it would look bad on him. Obviously, there is something wrong with his teaching—or the test."

The secret feeling, hope even, is that by force of the majority it will all work out. When by the thousands the Jews were packed into the trains, any sense of impending doom was diminished by the sheer numbers—"They can't kill us all." We are schooled in a lax society where standards are not viewed as absolute but rather as relative to the majority opinion. Yet we all live with uneasiness because we intuitively know we are failing God's humanity test.

It's like a recent situation in Britain. The people were failing their auto license tests in such large numbers that there was a public outcry, demanding test standards be lowered. When the head of the department, the man responsible for the tests, was directed to take his own test, he also failed. The people were delighted and the test standards were lowered. When we challenge God on the difficulty of His standards, our secret feeling is that if He took his own test under the same circumstances, He would fail also.

The arrogance of the human race is astounding. We presume to offer compromise deals to God. That which has the appearance of surrender to God is actually just *selling out* to a "Higher Power." We so much as say, "If you can be of assistance to me in the fulfillment of my personal goals, then I will have 'faith' and be religious." But, when our ambitions are thwarted we turn against our benefactor. The more devout, out of fear, are often driven to strike a bargain, giving up one sin or another on the chance that the Governor of all the Earth may grant a stay of execution.

What is now just a stalemate could in the days of eternity become a tragedy if petty pride keeps us from resolving our estrangement from our Maker. Like an emotionally wounded marriage partner, puffed up in pride, waiting for overtures from the other, we could wait to our own destruction. As the neglected marriage partner, God might just find happiness without us.

The Bible represents pride as the damning sin. When we consider the fact that the one with whom we are in controversy is Almighty God, it should make us doubt the validity of our doubts.

Trust or blame?

All of life involves trust. Trust is based on assumptions about the character of the other person. We are often uninformed as to the reason for one's actions. Where it concerns those for whom we have a great deal of respect, we have learned to suspend judgment until we have the full story. On the other hand, if it involves someone whom we are biased against, we are quick to impute an evil motive. During that period when the facts are obscure our response is not determined by our understanding but by our predisposition toward that person. Could it be that for personal reasons some find it convenient to lay the blame on their Creator? Have we, the human race, ever demonstrated a tendency to pass the blame? Are we guilty of misreading or misrepresenting the facts in our own personal relationships?

Personal conflicts may be dealt with by divorcing one's spouse or leaving one's family, job, or country. But when one divorces God he divorces life and sanity. There is no alternative to a relationship with God—only despair.

Chapter Eight
Accountability

Day of accounting

As surely as we are aware of our eventual death, we are aware the Creator will call each of us into account for this life. Even the most "primitive" peoples, isolated in remote jungles, are conscious of a day of reckoning with their Maker. This knowledge has been to all peoples a source of dread and sometimes stark fear. The more sophisticated cultures develop philosophies or religious systems of denial. Yet, when men linger at death's door, regardless of their professed beliefs, unless their consciences have been seared, true instincts dominate and they fear the coming judgment.

Resident judge — guilt

The judge that causes universal guilt is residing within each of us. It is inevitable that we should judge ourselves in regard to our own moral conduct and character. We have a built-in court system, an inner divine judge—the intellect enlightened by the human spirit. As we reflect on our own existence we eventually consider our place in the scheme of things. The image of God within testifies to our moral duty. If we have violated this innate sense of moral duty, we involuntarily blame ourselves. We call this self-accusation *guilt*.

We may formulate philosophies and state our unbelief in rational terms. Others attack their own brains with hypnosis and shock treatment. Some come to depend on mind-altering drugs. Many immerse themselves in religion, but no endeavor frees us from the finger of conscience. When men awake form chemical stupors and the inebriation of riotous pleasures the conscience is still pressing its finger against the nerve center of the soul.

Though we may deny future accountability, we all have an inner witness that is in agreement with moral law—as seen in our judgment of others. For when another commits a transgression, our response is to judge him according to the very rules we have denied. How many times have we heard of one committing a really vile crime, and we responded by a wish that he would meet his own just end in death? The judgment we apply to others is the truth of what we really believe. It is a hollow defense to deny accountability when we are holding others accountable. That is why the Scripture tells us we will be judged as we have judged others. While we are excusing our sins, our conscience is condemning us. While with our mind we are building our alibi for sin, our "resident divine judge" is building an airtight case to prosecute us.

If we were to perform up to the level at which we know ourselves to be capable, we would never suffer self-incrimination (guilt). It is only when we feel that we are blameworthy that we blame ourselves. The nature of the conscience is such that it never generates blame it does not believe it deserves. It is true that one may have a false notion about his guilt in a matter. Nevertheless, the subconscious mind will faithfully accuse according to its perception of right and wrong. All guilt is self-inflicted. It is internal and involuntary. Therefore, our guilt is a most accurate barometer of our true convictions.

Conscience

Many people think of the conscience as if it were a soulish organ—something independently functioning within. The conscience is not some appendix to the soul. It is that function of the intellect in its capacity for self-awareness and moral evaluation. The conscience is the man knowing himself. This involuntary part of our self-consciousness, functioning on a level deeper than our emotions, is difficult to deceive. As I am conscious of my existence, I am conscious of my duty. I am equally conscious of just how morally earnest I am in the performance of that duty. When I choose a course of action that is selfish I involuntarily blame myself. By means of my emotions and will I can lie with my mouth, but my spirit in the inner man knows the truth. When a man calls himself an atheist he is not attacking God, he is attacking his own conscience.

Life is a race in which each of us is a contestant. Death is the finish line. We are not competing against one another, and finishing the course does not make us winners. It is how we run the race that determines the score. There is no second place. We begin the race at that point in our youth when moral consciousness first begins to dawn. The race starts out slowly but quickly picks up pace as we get into the teen years. The rules are written in our inner consciousness. We are our own spectator, coach, and critic. We watch ourselves perform and we offer ideas to improve the performance, sometimes making resolutions. When we judge our performance to be below our own expectations, privately we become our strongest critics. We involuntarily point the finger of conscience at our own failure and then slump in guilt.

One incontrovertible truth is that we are all conscious of having failed in our moral duty. The whole world stands guilty, condemned by a judge within and in dread of the Judge without. If the secret conscience of the world could be photographed we would see its head bowed and its face hidden; yet, when seen in public it is standing proudly, head held high.

Our own consciences have judged us unfit to stand in the company of our Maker. Just as a young girl arriving home from committing her first fornication would be ashamed to sit across the table from her virtuous mother, so we would be ashamed to sit across the table from God.

Religion

Like a lonely man who settled for an empty house instead of a wife and family, many have settled for religion instead of God. Religion is the corporate activity of guilt-laden persons seeking restitution to whatever God or gods they may choose. Multiplicity of religion is testimony to the deep undeniable longing of the soul to be at peace with God. Few claim to have come away satisfied. It seems to be more of a quest than a school with graduates. Religion systematizes righteousness into do's and don'ts. The different religions are like different paths all leading to the same place—compounded guilt and death. Guilt is a great motivator—though not a very intelligent one.

Many are running the religious race, not knowing that all of humanity has already been individually disqualified. It was a false start. Our religious activities are in vain. The state into which our rebellion and selfishness has brought us is hopeless. The character we have molded for ourselves will forever disqualify us from communion with The Eternal.

The death sentence

Every mature human has indulged his flesh to the point of illicit gratification. For that reason the whole world is under a death sentence. This is not a penalty arbitrarily imposed by a vengeful judge exacting his due. The wages of sin is death, not because an angry God says so, rather, God says so because by nature it is so. Death is the natural consequence of sin.

Theoretically, if God should forsake and ignore the universe and never bother with us again, the wages of sin would still be death. It is not the man that put the label on the bottle who does the killing; it is the poison in the bottle. When we sin we incur the inherent penalty. God is our light and heat. Sin separates from God, and the cooling process begins. God does not freeze-out the sinner. When the man forsakes the light and heat he freezes in the darkness of his own making.

Only righteousness is self-perpetuating. Sin is like a malignant tumor; it will eventually destroy itself by destroying its host. Evil by nature tends toward disorder and progressive self-destruction. The nature of sin being what it is, the nature of the penalty could not be different from what it is. Sin would self-destruct even without judicial involvement. But God's role is to manage the consummation of sin so as to manifest the dignity of His office and the justice and glory of His righteousness. It is not just for His sake but for the good of all creation that God oversees the application of penal law.

Chapter Nine
Repentance

Reconciliation

Can anything be done, or is it too late? Is reconciliation still possible? For reconciliation to occur we must acknowledge that we are the offending party. We have been out of step with the program. Our disinterest must end. To be indifferent is not the same as being neutral. Indifference in a relationship is an insult, a statement of how little we value the other person. God deserves our supreme attention and energies because of the value of His contribution to those things that are of value. God values and cares for all things according to their worth. When all is in submission to the wisdom of His leadership, it can only result in the accomplishment of the supreme good for all. If we do not value God and the things He values, we do not value what we ought. If we eat, breathe, take up space, and don't live for a cause higher than our own pleasure, we are in opposition to goodness—to God.

We hear the sentiment expressed: "If God will leave me lone, I will leave Him alone." It is not as if there is an isolated corner of the universe where we can carry on our self-centeredness without any social ramifications. We are ever in the presence of the infinite God. Our indifference or rejection is a constant affront, not just to his person, but to the morale of the universe. To ride in the boat and not row is to impede the progress. *though we carry those who are weary*

Further, if we would be reconciled to God, we must deeply desire goodness of spirit and deed. More than we anticipate our daily food, we must come to continually desire holiness of temperament and action. The Bible says we are to *"thirst and hunger after righteousness."* We must reverse all forms of resistance to God and become active seekers of His will. To seek

God and desire His holiness is not self-reclamation. Seeking God is not the price tag of salvation. The only way a relationship can be restored is for both parties to desire it. The first step is to recognize our need and to desire God for who He is, to desire Him for His nature and His government. To desire God for personal reasons is not to desire God at all. It is nothing more than a desire for Divine assistance in the achievement of one's personal rebellion.

The thought patterns that resulted in distrust of our Creator must be swept away by the light of truth. Where there is not absolute trust there can be no respect, and certainly no commitment. To trust God is to turn to Him in confidence. To recognize our moral disease and turn to God as the cure is called "repentance." Jesus said, *"except ye repent, ye shall all likewise perish (Luke 13:3)."*

Repent (generally defined)

When you hear the word *repent* you may conjure up images of a gaunt prophet screaming doom if the world does not amend its ways. Though this would be an accurate usage of the word, it is not the way the Bible uses it in reference to reconciliation. Let us take an objective look at the word *repent*.

The verb *repent* was at one time quite common in everyday language, but its popularity in religion has caused it to fall out of common usage. Regardless of the contemporary connotation, it is by no means an exclusively religious word. Its Biblical usage is clearer when we understand its common meaning.

In the common sense, each of us repents many times every day. When we change our mind or actions in regard to anything, secular or sacred, we have repented.

Viewing repentance in its natural usage

- To an Artist, repentance could be to change the subject matter of the painting.
- To the Lover, repentance would be to change the one who is loved.
- To the Scientist, repentance could be to throw out the old theory and found his hypothesis on entirely new concepts.

- A child who has said, "Leave me alone; I can do it by myself," and then humbly seeks assistance, has repented.

- The teenager who at first refuses to cut the grass and then afterward does so has repented.

- When a man restructures his business under entirely new management, he has repented.

- When a traveler switches his destination, he repents.

- When a student changes his major, he repents.

- When the rebel lays down his arms and decides to participate in the political process, he repents.

- When the farmer plows under an immature crop and plants a different one, he has repented.

Focus of repentance

Repentance in its common usage is a different color, a different song, a different subject, a different belief, a different motivation. It is a new direction, a new purpose, a new goal, a new center around which everything revolves. It is a change of direction, feeling, doing, believing, etc. It is the reverse, the opposite, the other, as designated by its context.

Any given repentance has a focus, a direction, and a subject. The focus is not inherent within the word itself. *Repent* is an action word. To say *repent* without attaching an object or subject to it is to say nothing more than *turn, reverse*. One must ask, "Turn where? From what and to what should I turn?"

- If we are talking about beliefs, we would say, "Repent *from* your beliefs." We have given a command to turn and have defined the nature of the turn. It is to be a turn in regard to what you believe. Since there are many alternatives to any belief, in this case we have not implied what belief one is to repent *toward*.

- If we are talking about emotion, we might command, "Repent *from* your hatred." Again we have defined the turning as *away* from hate, and since there is an obvious alternative to hate, we have implied that the turn should be *from* hate *toward* love.

- If we are talking about actions, we could command, "Repent *from* the thing you are doing." We have not implied what action should take its place. Passivity is all that is implied.
- The Prophet might command, "Repent from your idolatry, and turn to the living God." The turn is defined as both *from* idolatry and *toward* God. Yet, if the prophet's command had been only, "Repent of your idolatry," we would have understood it to be repentance *toward* the God of the prophet.

Out of convenience or preference, there are many areas in which we might repent every day. And in the moral realm, there are many areas in which we should repent. But there is one particular repentance God has declared to be imperative.

New birth repentance

The repentance God requires for reconciliation is: *"repentance toward God (Acts 20:21)."* The direction and subject of the turn are defined as *"toward God."* There are other subjects of repentance in the Scripture, but the one required for reconciliation has God as the focal point of our turn. *Repentance toward God* is a refocusing of our life to a new source, a reversal of our concept as to the very purpose for existence. It is an undoing of Adam's decision to live independently of his Maker.

To and from

We have seen that in any repentance when one turns *toward* something, he is of necessity turning *from* something. The Scripture is clear in defining that *from* which one must repent when repenting *toward* God. When we repent toward God we are repenting from *"dead works (Heb. 6:1)."* Why is the other side of "repenting toward God" said to be "repenting from *dead works*" and not "repenting from sin?" Because sin itself is just the fruit of our independence from God. It is our spirit of independence and rebellion that is vying with God for preeminence. When we seek a path of good works in hopes of pleasing God, the vanity of our independent effort reduces the good works to *dead works*. Like a drowning man, it is our own flailing efforts to save ourselves that prevents someone else from saving us.

Minimal demand

To repent toward God is a most reasonable condition for reconciliation. It is a minimal demand. To turn *to* God is to turn *from* previous disinterest or neglect. Or, in the situation where one holds to a false belief that is a rival to God, to turn *to* God would be contemporaneous with turning *from* this false hope. The opposite of *repentance toward God* is indifference, preoccupation with personal activities that captivate our attention more than God. Or, clinging to some false belief system would be the opposite of repentance toward God.

God demands to become the focus of our life. To repent toward God is to fully turn to Him as not only the primary but also the singular concern. To repent *TOWARD* God is to repent *FROM* our independence of Him.

To repent toward God involves a cessation of hostilities; we no longer blame God for our plight. It is to believe that the answer to our moral condition is to be found in God alone. It is to weigh all of life's commitments and to regard God not merely at the top of the list but as the very fiber of all our being. It would not only be unreasonable but irrational for God to require less.

True repentance

True repentance is not a sentiment. It is not merely a *desire* to be right with God. An experience of deep religious passion is often mistaken for repentance. Tears and sorrow do not constitute repentance. True repentance transplants our heart in God's garden. It surrenders up the command of the soul to the Creator of the soul. True repentance takes root in Jesus Christ. It is the relationship of the branch to the vine.

True repentance is not an event in one's history; it is the beginning of a new history. It is not something you do once; it is a relationship into which you enter. It is the point at which life begins and the conscious footing on which it continues. After we have repented to God (God has become the center of our focus), God Himself will lead us into repenting from our habits of sin. Though repentance has God as its focus, and not sin, one can be sure that a union with God will immediately displace all known sin.

False repentance

When a lover professes to have a new love but continues to give attention to his old loves, his insincerity is clearly made manifest. He may plead with his professed new love that he is just a victim of his own weakness, that he is trying very hard to be faithful in his commitment to her, but that there are times when he still finds the old loves so attractive that he "gives them more attention than he knows he should." At such times he feels "very sorry" for his breaches of faithfulness. He deeply desires to repent of the old girl friends; he is just overcome by the passions of his flesh. We are not fooled. Clearly the man does not have a new love. He is simply attempting to pattern his new relationship according to what should be rather than that which is actually in his heart.

Many people become convinced of the wisdom of turning to God. They decide it is the right thing to do but find other pleasures more appealing. Their better judgment will cause them to confess a turn to God while they continue to love the former pleasures. That kind of "repentance" makes them no more of a Christian than it does a rich man. Many people desire to be rich who are not. The focus of new-birth repentance is not turning from something but rather turning *toward God*. To deeply desire to turn to God, even with sorrowful tears, is not the same as doing so.

Repenting from sins

Many stop short of repenting *TOWARD* God by becoming preoccupied with repenting *FROM* their sins. Knowing that repentance toward God will bear the fruit of repentance from sin, many have entrapped themselves in a syndrome of continually trying to be repentant of all sin in order to convince themselves, and perhaps God, that they are indeed His children. A man who has engaged himself in *repenting from his sins* in hope that he might validate his acceptance with God is like a sick man trying to get over the symptoms so he can prove he was cured last week. If he makes himself well before taking the medicine then he didn't need it. If he makes himself well after taking the medicine then it did him no good. He is trying to be his own doctor and savior.

In actuality he has put himself in the position of needing to repent of his repentance in order to be repentant toward God. He has replaced *repentance toward God* with the dead work of repentance from sins. In taking it upon himself to grapple with the sin that is sinking him, he is like a drowning man inhaling so he can blow out the water.

Those who analyze their turning and give great attention to it will never turn to God. They will continue to turn *from...* until they finally fail in abject spiritual exhaustion. God is the source of a new life, not the goal of our repentance. He accepts us so He might give us a new life; He does not give us new life so that He might accept us. When a man has assumed the responsibility (albeit with God's help) of repenting from his sins as a condition to being acceptable to God, he has engaged in the ultimate act of futility.

Concerning reconciliation, it is not the habits of sins from which we must turn, rather, from the heart of independence and neglect of our Creator. When we give God rightful place in our hearts His presence will eventually displace the sin. The issue is one of relationship, not personal condition. The condition of sin is the symptom; the broken relationship is the disease. Sin's condition is only cured after we are in fellowship with God.

The psychological need to repent from sins

Being in the image of God, we intuitively feel God's aversion to sin. Deep within, we know that He cannot fellowship with iniquity. We know the breach has been caused by our willful sinfulness. It therefore seems reasonable to assume that since He rejected us because of sin He will receive us back only if we stop sinning. We also know that if the breach was originally caused by sin, to bring sin into the restored relationship would constitute further grounds for a continuing breach. It is universally unthinkable—and rightly so—that a man could come back to God while persisting in the sin that originally caused the separation. It is from this very knowledge that we stray into error.

Perhaps I can illustrate it this way: If a married man was kicked out of the house for taking up with a girlfriend, he would not have the boldness to return seeking restitution unless he repented *from* the girlfriend. He would never consider seeking restitution with the girlfriend still in tow. Since it was grounds to get him kicked out in the first place, it would remain a detriment to reconciliation.

Furthermore, the degree to which the man respects his wife is the degree to which he feels the necessity of repenting from his girlfriend as a condition for reconciliation. If he should have the audacity to boldly return with the girlfriend, he would be further insulting and demeaning the wife whom he has spurned. All of this the man intuitively knows without ever giving it deliberate thought. With him it is not a doctrine that requires religious devotion to maintain. It is a basic psychological presupposition that no one would ever consider challenging.

A case against my position? So, it seems I have built a case against my own position. Does my illustration support the widely held assumption that the condition for reconciliation is to stop sinning? Let us look at the example more closely. What I have above described is the prodigal's perspective, not the wife's. The sinner's psychological inclinations will ever remain the same in any relationship where repentance is called for. But what we are seeking is the nature of repentance from God's perspective (represented by the wife in our illustration), not the sinner's.

If the wife desired reconciliation with the unfaithful husband, on what grounds would she accept his return? The apparent answer is to say that he must give up the girlfriend. But no, the wife expects something much deeper. To merely grieve over the consequences of his unfaithfulness and desist from the girlfriend would never, in the mind of the offended wife, constitute solid grounds for reconciliation. From the wife's perspective it is not just that he chose the girlfriend but that he 'unchose' her. She demands that he turn his heart back to her, that he becomes consumed with love for her, the wife of his youth, that he desires her first, foremost and only. It would not be enough for him to just repent from the girl friend. He must first repent *toward* his wife. The wife knows that if she has his heart she will have everything else, including his faithfulness.

God is greatly offended over our sin, but to cease sinning would not rectify the relationship. It was not that Adam ate one piece of fruit that caused a total loss of fellowship, but that in eating he rejected God.

God desires that all men repent from their lecherous affair with sin, but He knows from history that men will make a religion of their repentance from sins and still not face their heart problem. Though it is a minimal expectation to require us to cease sinning, God, knowing the futility of such a condition, has invited us to come while still in our sins. That does not mean that God has invited us to bring sin into the relationship, but that the invitation to come to him is fully extended while we are still in captivity to the sin itself. We come to him with our sin, not that we might continue in it, but that upon being received by God we might be freed from the sin.

He knows that the flesh is weak and that we have so indulged ourselves in sin that we are made captive to our lusts. Receiving the sinner while still in his sin is not an indication that God has lowered His moral standards, but He knows His forgiveness and presence will work a process that will free the sinner from sin. God also knows that the image of God within us will not be satisfied with anything short of a just and honorable unconditional surrender.

Though God desires us to stop sinning, being psychologically enslaved as we are, He has not made it a precondition. He has challenged us with His already provided forgiveness. He demands only that we repent to Him with all our heart. When He gets our heart, He has the whole person, from the inside out.

God has not made Himself estranged, waiting for us to assume the initiative in repentance. But in His jealousy for us He has gone on the offensive to regain our faithfulness. God has responded like a wife who, forsaken for a cheap girlfriend, decides to seek restoration of the wanderer. Knowing the power of guilt to keep the unfaithful husband estranged, she doesn't wait for him but goes into the den of iniquity to remind the fallen husband that he will be forgiven if he will return. She is inviting him to repent back to her. If she had gone with a message of "give her up or else," he would not be moved to repentance. But a message of "I welcome you back home" can move him to *repent toward* her pure love and forgiveness.

As with God, her aggressive invitation is not designed to provide a less than honorable grounds for reconciliation; it is designed to move him to a broken heart that longs to be secure in a just and pure love. In not mentioning his sin, she understands, and he understands, that the condition for reconciliation is to repent back to his wife, which will result in repentance from every potential rival.

She need not fear that her "grace" invitation will result in his coming home with the girlfriend still in tow, for she knows that his own conscience has already judged the two opposing choices (the wife and the girlfriend) to be mutually exclusive. In his mind, as it should be, it is an either/or choice.

Some would protest, **"But if repentance to God always results in repentance from sin, then are they not the opposites of one act? Can we not look to the repentance from sin as a sure barometer of repentance toward God?"** Absolutely not! To do so is to create a reverse order that puts the focus on the effect rather than the cause. It is to place a responsibility upon the sinner which he rightly deserves but will never have the courage to completely perform. Repentance from sin will become the fruit of a restored relationship only when we focus on the relationship and not the fruit.

Returning to our illustration: If she focuses on his giving up the girlfriend, he will only struggle with his passions until he drowns in his own weaknesses. But if she presents herself as the object of his repentance (affection), then in focusing on her his passion for the girl friend will fade into insignificance. As he repents *toward* the faithful, forgiving wife, he will repent *from* not only this one woman but all others as well—including any future potential rivals.

Even with the universal, innate need to repent of sins, God desiring it, religion demanding it, and our most striving efforts to do so, the fact is no one has ever repented from all sin. We have either excused our sins, collapsed in remorse, or offered some feeble form of restitution to the offended Deity.

Chapter Ten
The Restraints of Guilt

On a practical level

If a man did indeed repent toward God it would be the reversal of Adam's move to independence—in which case, certainly God would be pleased. But on a practical level, apart from the ministry of the Holy Spirit, in reality men do not repent toward God. To repent toward God would involve a complete conversion of attitude and intent, whereas one could repent of his sins without turning to God. But history has proven that we sinners are too morally depraved to make a complete and entire break. Whether repentance toward God or repentance from sins, our best endeavors have proven to be only partial.

Again, keep in mind, our inability does not lie in human nature. As we have discussed, we have the constitutional ability to repent from any sin, as well as the ability to repent toward God. Yet, for reasons that are personal and in a sense original with each sinner, all human repentance falls short of total admission of guilt. Any confessions we make are designed to advantage us. A prominent figure caught in immorality will weep publicly and thereby regain a measure of respectability. A tormented conscience finds release in confession and restitution. A man caught in violation of public law will confess his deed in hope of receiving mercy. If a man who smokes discovers that a cancer is forming in his lungs there is no merit in his quitting. It is purely selfish. A dead-works repentance from sin may be nothing more than saying, "I have done wrong, but now I have the wisdom and good intentions to do the right thing." There is no loss of self-esteem here and no genuine refocus. The self is still the motivation for that kind of repentance.

Why is it so difficult for us adult transgressors to admit blame? It is the rational and sane thing to do. The alternative is spiritual and physical self-destruction. Picture a situation in which you confront your child for wrongdoing. You are prepared to offer correction and forgiveness. It seems simple to you. You hope the child will just say, "I'm sorry; I messed up. I will not do it again." You will be delighted. The child will not be punished or even lectured. You will be more proud of him than if he had continued in obedience, for he has demonstrated a maturity of character. But what does the little tot do? He puts on a sincere convincing expression and denies any involvement. Or, if he deems the evidence to be irrefutable, he will give a trumped up excuse. As he gets older, he may defend his waywardness by challenging the standards or by questioning your moral authority to legislate. Why doesn't he just give-in to his conscience and admit his error? As the child, in a desire to save our reputation, we will turn away from the conviction before we will kneel to receive a pardon.

Hypocrites: As we get older and develop a reputation for being a good person, our aversion to repentance actually increases. A *reputation* of doing right can become more important than the *state* of being good. This is seen by our tendency to shift, quickly and hopefully unnoticed, to the side of right without acknowledging that we were ever wrong. It's the stuff of which hypocrites are made. Right-doing with a selfish motive is still the sin of selfishness. When confronted with our sin, the great sense of guilt causes us to respond exactly as Adam did. His shame caused him to hide from God. Adam blamed God for giving him the woman. The woman blamed the Serpent. To blame someone else is dishonest. It is not only unrepentant but impenitent as well.

What does all this denial and pretense tell us? It tells us that our esteem for righteousness causes such an aversion to facing our sinfulness that we would rather do anything than admit total blame. The more a man listens to his own inner witness, the more aware he becomes of his alienation from the righteous God. The awful sense of separation and self-loathing that sin brings causes a man to seek relief by denial—creating excuses.

Even those psychological wrecks that we are told are victims of self-loathing are actually angry at those circumstances that brought them to this disappointing self-analysis. They value that state of being right so much that they are emotionally distraught by the blame they inflict upon themselves. They may well dislike themselves, but not enough to repent. To repent would be to plunge deeper into self-judgment. The conscience screams its accusations at the mind, and the heart flees in disgust. They would allow sin to continue rather than accept responsibility for it.

Our pride will not allow us to admit we are sinful beggars until after we have taken commendable steps to rise from the gutter. It is easy to admit that you have failed—after you have made arrangements to succeed. On the other hand, repentance toward God is to say:

"I am a failure. I have no prospects for deliverance and no hope. I am morally wretched and undone. The Devil is my pimp, and I am a prostitute to sin, with insufficient motivation to quit. God help me, for I am an unclean and undone rebel and I deserve no respect. I am without honor. I have not only done wrong, I am wrong. I deserve to perish. It is all my fault. I now turn to God and plead for His most undeserved mercy."

Oh the release of a captive heart that truly repents to God!

The two insurmountables:

Two things within us must be satisfied before we will repent toward God.

One: We must have assurance that when we approach God He will receive us. We intuitively know that it is His duty to vanquish sin, and we feel this to be both just and appropriate. For that reason we are reluctant to approach where we fear to be rejected. The wondrous thing is how in our consciences we mirror His moral government. It is our self-conviction, agreement with His righteous standards, that keeps us estranged from God.

By our own guilt we have written for ourselves permanent papers of estrangement. God has sought us out and offered reconciliation based on our willingness to place ourselves in His care. But there remains in us the psychological barrier, based on our respect for God, that will not allow us to believe we are accepted unless we know that we are repentant in heart toward God.

By way of illustration: The king appointed a day for all those guilty of treason to come forward and receive a pardon. As one traitorous wretch walked toward the palace, his fear of incrimination increased with each step. As he came within sight of the palace, the thought of the shame he would feel when standing before the king was so overwhelming that he turned and fled. He resolved instead to simply reform his ways and in the future live in a fashion that would be acceptable to the king. With the passing of years the guilt and fear of being discovered tormented his soul. He had repented of his treason, but he had not repented toward the king.

We are drowning in a psychological quagmire of our own making. We have been thrown the life-ring of repentance, but fear of being rejected by the very one who would save us has caused us to maintain a grip on the sinking debris of our own wrecked conscience. We will not release a frail object that offers a little hope—like self-effort—until we have embraced a more promising salvation. Nor will we lay down our excuses, entering the dark tunnel of blame and guilt, until we see the light of acceptance at the other end. In other words, until we have confidence that God will forgive us, we will not repent to Him. For that reason, only some initiative on God's part will bring men to repentance, not because we are constitutionally unable to repent, but because our selfishness and pride render us spiritually unwilling.

Two: Before we can be induced to repent toward God we must be satisfied that we are coming to Him with a just and acceptable offering for sin. To reform our ways from this point forward does not cleanse our conscience. We wholeheartedly believe that sin does deserve death. The sins of the past are not atoned for by future obedience. We know that tomorrow has its own requirements of righteousness. We already owe to God all future acts of obedience. We subconsciously know that past blame is not removed by the future obedience. At the time we did wrong there was no justification for our actions. We know ourselves to still be that person. Thus we involuntarily take up the scepter of moral government and stand with God to condemn ourselves.

We are like rogues of the night who sleep in the day, never seeing the filth of our moral attire. When we consider returning to the people of the light, we become more conscious of the dirt on our person. Should we actually make an attempt to surface into the world of the clean, the closer we draw to the light the more loathsome we feel. The shame and guilt finally drive us back to our self-ordained captivity. We need to be clean, and we need assurances that we will be accepted by Him whom we have rejected and offended.

We, being in the image of God, cannot rest where justice is not done. We cannot believe in forgiveness founded on the will of God alone, for we would forever feel burdened with the guilt of our transgression. Our nature being in the image of God, we cannot dismiss the penalty of sin. This moral nature will not lay aside guilt until it has met its just due. The nature of man requires atonement, and repentance will not occur without it.

So the stage is set with two principal characters estranged from each other by the infidelity of the lesser. The lesser has considered seeking reconciliation but has been turned back by aversion to the intense light of exposure. The estranged God is bound by the same laws that govern their common natures. He is responsible to oversee the termination of evil and to satisfy all legal considerations.

Legal considerations

As we have pointed out, sin has an inherent penalty—death. God has the power but not the right to set aside the penalty of sin. To do so would go against common law. It would be to act contrary to His own nature, as well as ours. As we have seen above, our own consciences would not allow a reconciliation that was not just. He would be unjust to forgive without first meeting the law's demand—that law being common in the nature of all beings. His own just nature demands that evil be exterminated. For God not to rise up in righteous judgment against sin would make Him an accomplice. It is His moral duty to preside over the court of justice in retribution toward all elements of rebellion.

As moral governor of the universe, God is responsible to govern justly. If He would maintain the public's expectation of integrity in moral government—if, in the future, the law is to have any meaning, if the moral law of cause and effect is to remain operative, if the damned are to see that the justice of God has been equally applied to all, then there must be a just and worthy accounting for sin. The law's demand must be met, even for the repentant.

The sum of our need

Here is the sum of the matter: The Creator is found still loving His fallen creatures, but due to their moral condition He is unable to persuade the sometime arrogant, sometime trembling souls to repent. And if they did He could not justly forgive them. The nature of moral consciousness and legal justice being as inflexible as it is, the dilemma seems to have no solution.

Job said, *"If I justify myself, mine own mouth shall condemn me: If I say, I am perfect, it shall also prove me perverse (Job 9:20)."* Then he contemplates his estrangement from God, saying, *"For he is not a man, as I am, that I should answer him, and we should come together in judgment. Neither is there any daysmen* [someone to act as arbitrator in settling differences] *betwix us, that might lay his hand upon us both (Job 9:32-33)."* Job, being aware of the chasm between himself and God, in desperation cried out his longing for a mediator *("daysmen")*. Someone was needed to function as a go-between—to legally and justly represent the best interest of both parties.

Chapter Eleven
The GOD-MAN Between

Legal counsel

From before the foundation of the world God's Son was elected to become the mediator. A mediator must have the credentials to mediate in the presence of both parties. The Infinite is limited to His infiniteness and cannot intimately know the finite except by some process of self-diminishing, some self-imposed limitations. He must create Himself finite. This He did in the womb of a Jewish virgin.

He who was with God and was God separated Himself from the Father and could yet say, *"If you have seen me, you have seen the Father." "Great is the mystery of godliness;"* for while He was separate from the Father in heaven He professed to have come from and said He would return to the Father. But at the same time that Jesus was seen among men, God in heaven called the Son on earth *"The Everlasting Father."* We are told that the worlds were created by the Son of God. But when the time was right, God the son entered the finite world through the veil of mortal flesh and blood.

It would seem that if the plight of man was a curse then the Creator had sentenced Himself to the same. His human body was subject to the same frailties as ours. He grew weary and hungry, required sleep, and would bleed when cut. He was lured, unsuccessfully, by every sin known to man. As a mortal His only defense was the Spirit and Word of God, along with learned wisdom concerning good and evil.

Champion of righteousness

Where the rest of the human race failed, this man Jesus took up the law and prevailed against all temptation. This one, lone human being stood up under the full weight of temptation until Satan fled in defeat. By succeeding where all others had failed, the championship of righteousness passed to this one son of man.

Through his perfect obedience He earned the right for one of humanity's own to be seated at the right hand of the Father. At last a man had qualified to hold divine office. Through His knowledge as overcomer He qualified to assume the position of legal counselor and advocate. Further, in His body of flesh as an overcomer He prepared Himself to assume all liabilities, obligations, and debts of those whom He was to represent.

Read his press releases

- The Father said of Him: *"This is my beloved Son, in whom I am well pleased (Matt. 3:17)."*

- He said of Himself: *"For I do always those things that please him (John 8:29)."*

- One who spent three-and-one-half years with Him said: *"We beheld his glory, the glory as of the only begotten of the Father, full of grace and truth (John 1:14)."*

- An apostle said of Him: He was *"in all points tempted like as we are, yet without sin (Heb. 4:15)."*

- Pilate, His enemy, said: *"I find no fault in this man (Luke 23:4)."* And, as if in challenge to the whole world, Pilate presented to the public this man whom he had declared innocent, and then he announced, *"Behold the man (John 19:5)!"*

As we behold the man, we see a man as God intended him to be. He didn't just obey the law; He fulfilled it. The heretofore-unreachable law held up its measuring stick. He accepted the challenge and quickly broke all records of righteousness, soaring so far beyond all, that the law humbly bowed, retiring in His presence. In Him humanity reached unprecedented heights. The standard was raised. The law became obsolete and stood aside for one more righteous.

- Of all mankind, only one is holy: *"the holy One of Israel" (Isa. 17:7)."*
- *"Who shall ascend into the hill of the Lord? or who shall stand in his holy place? He that hath clean hands, and a pure heart; who hath not lifted up his soul unto vanity, nor sworn deceitfully (Psalm 24:3-4)."*
- He is *"holy, harmless, undefiled, separate from sinners, and made higher than the heavens (Heb. 7:26)."*
- He is elected by God because He *"loved righteousness and hated iniquity (Heb. 1:9)."*
- He is the one and only Man who *"descended"* and was so untouched by human sin that He qualifies to *"ascend"* up far above all things and to be *"seated at the right hand of the Majesty on high (Eph. 4)."*

At the end of a life of testing, unmarked by the stain of sin, there walked a perfect man worthy to sit in the presence of God or to stand at the head of the human race. He could have ascended back into the heavens, fulfilling the Father's desire, for human companionship. But according to plan this one, overcoming Son of Man chose to represent the human race under the heel of Divine judgment.

Jesus made to be sin

After a life of full obedience Jesus went to an appointed garden at an appointed time and by faith knelt to receive upon Himself the sins of the entire world. The Father *"laid on Him the iniquity of us all."* He *"became sin for us"* and carried our transgressions to the hill of death. When He was nailed to the cross God viewed it as if every person who would ever live was potentially nailed for payment of sin. The punishment necessary to make peace for everyone was put upon Him.

The law of our very being demanded death to the sinner. Christ received our sins and died as the representative sinner. Since He was a perfect man He could be a suitable substitute for sinful men. Since He was infinite God the merit of His substitution could be infinitely applied.

To paraphrase a well-worn statement from a former age: God loved the people of the earth so much that He gave His only son to suffer in the place of sinning souls. The way is now cleared for all those who would believe God to have the merit of that deed applied to their own account. Those who believe will never suffer the just consequences of death but will receive a new life that will never end. See John 3:16 in the King James Bible for the original.

By resisting all temptation, Christ demonstrated His power over sin. By raising bodies from the dead, He demonstrated His power over death. By casting out devils, He demonstrated His power over Satan. Sin, death, and Hell had no hold over this one man. And then, like Isaac, He lay down on the altar to become the sin offering.

A sinner by faith

Kneeling in the garden, Jesus believed God and received the weight of sin. God *"made him to be sin for us, who knew no sin, that we might be made the righteousness of God in him (2 Cor. 5:21)."* God was willing to see Jesus as a sinner that He might be permitted to see us as righteousness. Jesus became what we are that we might become what He is. By the imputing act of God, He became a sinful son of man so we could become sinless sons of God. It was a trade. He traded His righteousness for our sin. He then bore the consequences of our sin before God so that we can bear the consequences of His righteousness before God. He ascended the hill of Calvary so we could ascend Mount Zion. The God who *"calleth those things which be not as though they were"* called His Son something He wasn't—a sinner—so that He could call us something we are not—righteous. *"Blessed is the man to whom the Lord will not impute sin (Rom. 4:82)."*

For those who believe, God sees no sin except that which is upon Jesus. God therefore punished the man Jesus until the penalty of our sin was exhausted and the justice of the law was fully satisfied.

Under the curse

Jesus hung on the cross, not as the accepted man, but as the cursed and rejected man. The human race was a mountain of condemned flesh. Jesus climbed to the top of the pile and received into his body the full blast of all God's fury. He alone knows what it is to fall into the hands of the living God bearing the full penalty of sin. The curse of the law poured into Jesus until it was empty; then the sword of justice was broken off in His holy flesh.

Resurrected

Under the watchful eye of the law He was lowered to hell carrying the sin of the world. The law walked away from the execution fully satisfied. Viewing His execution, it closed its case against all whom He represents.

But the Scripture quotes Jesus in that hour, *"For thou will not leave my soul in hell; neither wilt thou suffer thine Holy One to see corruption (Psalm 16:10)."*

When the justice of God and the demand of the law was fully expended, He exercised his rights as an overcomer and ascended, leaving the power of sin broken and death void of its sting.

A man who has paid for the crimes chargeable to him is released from prison. So God released the overcoming man from the prison house of death. In the resurrection, Jesus is the accepted M●, received into glory, seated on God's right hand in eternal fellowship with the Father.

Imputed righteousness

The God-man had paid the full debt of sin that was demanded by all moral beings. Everyone's sense of justice was satisfied in His substitution. Believing this to be true, the way is clear for us to repent toward God without fear of retribution.

God made Jesus to be sin: We now come to the sweetest truth of the gospel. Jesus was made sin in the same manner that we are made righteous. By faith Jesus knelt in the garden and received our sin. From that moment God viewed Jesus as if He were every sinner for all time. To be laden with our sin, Jesus simply knelt and by faith received sin on His body. In the same fashion, we receive His righteousness. Jesus did not do the sin that took Him to the cross, and we do not do the righteousness that takes us to heaven.

The sin that took Jesus to the cross was on Him only in God's accounting. Likewise, the righteousness that takes us to heaven is only in God's accounting. That is, it is not a personally lived righteousness. It is a vicarious righteousness. This saving righteousness was lived by one man only.

Through His obedience, all that believe are counted as if they were always fully obedient. In God's counting, the believer has never sinned. Rather, God has imputed to us the thirty-three and one-half years of Christ's obedience. As far as the heavenly records show, the believer is sinless; he has always obeyed God. The Father does not remember our sin. When God looks upon us it is through the righteousness of the man Christ Jesus. "I owed a debt I could not pay. He paid a debt He did not owe," that I might be reconciled in my conscience as well as in the court of heaven. Such knowledge moves me to repent toward my Creator/Savior.

Not enabling grace

The righteousness that saves is not the grace of God *enabling* us to do what we ought; it is the grace of God offering a *free gift* of righteousness. This righteousness is not lived out in our experience. It is like someone else's money that you never handled or saw, and yet it paid your debt. That is, it is a substitute righteousness, a provided gift of righteousness.

Substitute righteousness

As you stand before God, lacking the righteousness necessary to get into heaven, Jesus offers His righteousness to God as a substitute for yours. His righteousness doesn't just complete yours; it is a total substitute. I owe to God perfect holiness. If I fall short of that, I am forever hopeless before God. He cannot look upon anything other than perfect purity. The blood of Jesus Christ (His poured out life) removes the legal stain of my sin, and the righteousness of Jesus Christ is placed to my account. This righteousness is called *"imputed righteousness."* The cross and the blood of Jesus Christ absolve me of the penalty. The resurrection and righteousness of Jesus Christ guarantee my future.

The gift of righteousness

The apostle Paul said, *"And be found in him, not having mine own righteousness, which is of the law, but that which is through the faith of Christ, the righteousness which is of God by faith (Phil. 3:9)."* In Philippians 3:4-6, Paul describes his works and then says he counts them as dung. He does not profess to have personally attained (Phil. 3:13). He does not look to his righteousness, rather, he looks to the *"gift of righteousness"* to save him (Rom. 5:17). That gift was presented to the Father on our behalf, the gift that is now seated beside the Father. *"But of him are ye in Christ Jesus, who of God is made unto us wisdom, and righteousness, and sanctification, and redemption (1Cor. 1:30)."* Christ Himself is *"made"* our righteousness.

Righteousness without works

What does one do to have this righteousness imputed to his account? *"Even as David also describeth the blessedness of the man, unto whom God imputeth righteousness without works, Saying, Blessed are they whose iniquities are forgiven, and whose sins are covered. Blessed is the man to whom the LORD will not impute sin (Rom. 4:6)."* *"But for us also, to whom it shall be imputed, if we believe on him that raised up Jesus our Lord from the dead (Rom. 4:24)."* **"Believe"** is the condition. Read Romans 4-5 in the King James Bible.

"Sirs, what must I do to be saved? Believe on the Lord Jesus Christ, and thou shalt be saved (Acts 16:30-31)."

Parable of the king's son

In a faraway land and in another time, a benevolent king ruled his kingdom wisely, and all the people loved him. Well, not all. There was a small group of rebels who worked in secret, seeking to overthrow his rule. They wanted the freedom to engage in immoral revelry, which was not permitted under this righteous king. The usual punishment for treason was death, but the king passed a law saying that anyone guilty of treason would be allowed to live but would have his eyes put out. On several occasions young men were brought before the king to be tried for treason. After carefully hearing the evidence the king had regretfully pronounced the penalty of blindness upon some of these young men.

One day the king's sheriff brought a young man before the court to be tried for treason. It was rumored that he was the ringleader of the rebellion. The king was disturbed by the hood covering the upper body of the prisoner. But the court lawyers requested that the concealment remain in place to assure that justice would be accomplished. The king went along with the request, assuming that the accused must be an acquaintance or perhaps the son of some state official. He and heard the evidence that proved to be overwhelmingly incriminating. When it came time to pass sentence the lawyers removed the hood to reveal the king's own son. The king was about to pass the sentence of blindness on his only son. With great restraint of his emotions he announced that he would wait twenty-four hours to pronounce the judgment. Though it could not make a difference in the court's decision, the king used that time, to no avail, trying to bring his son to repentance. The son felt sure that the father could not forgive him, and the penalty of the law was unavoidable.

During the intervening time, word of the developing situation spread over all the kingdom. There was much speculation about what the king would do. Half of the people characterized the king as a man who placed duty and the letter of the law above his own feelings. They supposed the king would not only take out his son's eyes but also have him executed as an example. The other half of the kingdom believed the king would yield to deep feelings toward his son and free him unharmed. Many believed that he would elicit from the son a promise of allegiance and then set aside the penalty of the law.

The king found himself in a dilemma, with two conflicting compulsions. He desired to save his son, and he desired to remain a just and lawful king. Having blinded others for the same offense, could he make an exception with his son and still maintain the public perception of just? How could the public continue to respect his rule? Furthermore, if he should withhold the punishment, how could he command respect or control of his son? The offense would forever stand between the king and his son. If not punished, would the rebellious son not be even bolder in his rebellion?

On the other hand, how could he pass sentence on his own son? Could a father who begat a son of his own body, and invested so much in rearing him, suddenly shut off all feelings? Could he just blind his son and forget? Would life have any further meaning for a father?

Twenty-four hours later the court was reconvened. The royal city was packed with expectant, solemn onlookers. The prisoner was brought into the court. His face not being covered, his bitterness was clear for all to see. Looking at his countenance, one would think he was holding his father responsible for his rebellion.

The king was the last to enter the chamber. With expectancy running high, he was led into the chamber wearing the hood his son wore the day before. Feebly, he was steered to his place on the throne. He immediately commenced to recount the incriminating evidence. Then while the crowd stood in hushed wonder, just when he was preparing to pass sentence he reached up and slipped the hood from his head. The audience fell back in revulsion as they saw the two gaping, bloody holes where royal eyes had once been. The crowd gasped as the king addressed the general public. A servant placed before the people a tray containing the king's eyes. The king asked the general public if common justice could be served by the substitution of his eyes for his son's. The people unanimously agreed that justice was served. The king had found a way to be faithful to his law, thereby maintaining its integrity, and a way to satisfy his love to his son.

One problem remained, the son's rebellion. If the father had been able to elicit prior repentance from the son, the sacrifice would have seemed justifiable. But the offering was made when the son was still a self-proclaimed enemy of the king. That too was resolved in the king's bloody sacrifice. Seeing the father's love and forgiveness, the son was moved to repent toward his father. All doubt as to the father's love and wisdom involuntarily vanished. The son fell at his father's feet and begged for the forgiveness that he had already received. He was placed at the father's right hand where he forever thereafter faithfully and benevolently assisted in all affairs of the kingdom.

The dilemma was solved. Sacrificing neither his love to his son nor justice, the law had been honored in a way that elevated it as never before. The king had not only expressed his love to his son, but had brought him to humble repentance. The integrity of the kingdom was maintained and the son was saved—all at the father's expense. *"That he might be just and the justifier... For God so loved the world that he gave...."*

Chapter Twelve
The Gospel

The published truth

The law is what we should do. The gospel is what God has done in light of our failure to do what we ought. The gospel is not the process of God *making* us righteous, it is the act of Him *declaring* us righteous. Jesus Christ is erected before God as the full satisfaction of all the sinner's needs. He is offered to the sinner as the full satisfaction of all his needs.

The gospel is a declaration of a complete provision for the complete man with a complete need. Therefore, the gospel is not an offer of something that will come into existence if men respond, but it is the good news that something is already in existence that men might respond. God provides, then offers. We contemplate not our duty but the offer. The last move is ours—receive.

There are no conditions to entering the gospel's provision. Rather, the gospel is a declaration that the conditions have already been met; and as such, there can be no personal achievement. You cannot succeed before God; you can only joy in God's success, for the gospel comes as good tidings of a deed accomplished.

The sinner does not come to God; God comes to him when he believes. There is never cause to delay in believing. Any modifications we would make in personal preparation can only render us more unfit by adding the sin of pride to that of unbelief. *"Come unto me all ye that labour and are heavy laden, and I will give you rest,"* said the Savior.

The gift of righteousness is for those who *"worketh not, but believeth on him that justifieth the ungodly (Rom. 4:5)."* *"And be found in him, not having mine own righteousness, which is of the law, but that which is through the faith of Christ, the righteousness which is of God by faith (Phil. 3:9)."*

It's Your Move

Mankind's original sin began as distrust of the Creator. Reconciliation begins with a renewal of trust. To trust God is faith. To turn to God from other sources of trust is repentance. It is ours to do if we would be in fellowship with our Creator. As children believe their parents, we are expected to believe God.

Friendships are built on respect and trust. God trusted us to share His image and likeness. Then, when we dropped out of the program, He respected our right of privacy and individuality. Have we in turn trusted Him? Have we respected His plan for the Kingdom? Have we been worthy subjects? Reconciliation can only occur when we are in full sympathy with the program of God. In our finiteness there are things we will never know. It is only reasonable that in a spirit of cooperation we should trust God. Where there is no trust, there can be no love or cooperation. When you trust someone, you believe what he says. You are willing to take his word as reality. Where there is genuine deep love and trust, we are willing to believe the other person over the sight of our own eyes. As in any human relationship, God expects mutual cooperation and moral earnestness.

The Bible calls this state of trusting "belief." *"Without faith it is impossible to please him,"*— simply because faith is the ground of all person-to-person relationships. It is the foundation of any cooperative endeavor. God does not ask us to have a mountain moving faith—just a faith that puts Him at the center of our focus.

Thus, the one condition we must meet for reconciliation to occur is to *"believe God."* Belief is a two-sided coin. To say *"repent"* is to state our duty negatively. To say *"believe"* is to state our duty positively.

God in earnest

As the deposit of earnest money seals a bargain, God has given to His adopted children a down payment on the coming inheritance. Jesus said, *"And I will pray the Father, and he shall give you another Comforter, that he may abide with you forever: even the Sprit of truth: whom the world cannot receive, because it seeth him not, neither knoweth him: but ye know him; for he dwelleth with you, and shall be in you (John 14:16-17)."* The believer is not left to the power of faith. We now have more than the conscience and more than the written word for a guide; we have been given the presence of God Himself—the Holy Spirit.

Yipee!

Our future together

Death no longer has any hold on those of us that have been reconciled to God. Death is just a release from this limiting body of flesh and blood. Death is our graduation into our full inheritance. It is coming home to our Heavenly Father and His family. It is just the beginning of what life was intended to be.

Contrary to what many have supposed, we are not going to be turned out to pasture on a fluffy cloud where we will fiddle away eternity playing impractical little harps and fanning all-too-small wings. Nor are we destined to an eternal eleven o'clock church service with lectures on faithfulness, concluded by long pious prayers. No, passing into eternity is not confinement in a cloistered monastery in the sky; it is the release of a captive bird into a universe of discovery.

We will reside in a splendid city set on a new earth with trees, grass, rivers, sunshine, and animals in abundance. We will eat and drink, dance and sing. Possibly there will be new frontiers to conquer and new planets to fashion. We will continue to learn and to grow. The utopian dream will become reality.

Through the tutorship of the grace of God, the school of life here on earth, with all of its accompanying experiences, will have produced righteous children whom God is not ashamed to call *family*.

Faith that works

In a moment's time the believing sinner passes from death to life. But life doesn't end with salvation, it begins. Where there is new life, there is new living. This newness of life does not come forth from the new Christian because of a command that it should. It comes forth naturally because of the transplanted life of God in the new creature. We are so thankful for the gift of righteousness that we are moved to obey the Father in everything. We deeply desire to act like the sons of God that we are. Our holiness after salvation is the fruit of that gift of righteousness.

The next step: The faith that saves matures to become a working faith. We are part of His body and are engaged in the greatest work of all time, taking the good news to the whole world. If you personally discovered a cure for a dreaded, deadly disease, you would go to any expense and suffer any humiliation or loss to get that cure to those who needed it. After 2000 years many of earth's inhabitants have yet to hear of the Great Physician. They do not deserve to hear, but He deserves to be known.

One more time—a summary

- God desired persons with whom He could fellowship. To create the same it was necessary that the creature be in God's own image.

- To be in God's image of necessity requires that all aspects of God's nature be present, albeit on a smaller scale—from the infinite to the finite—of the same kind, though different in degree.

- Essential to personhood is mind, will, and emotions, made alive by the spirit. God-given personhood is by nature without external or internal physical restraints. That is, there are no controls over the choices that we make. Such control would render us non-human.

- By nature, each of us has an understanding of our moral duty. This does not need to be taught, and is seldom even spoken of. It is the moral image of God stamped on our inner being. By it we feel a duty to do the right. It is that universally accepted standard of moral conduct by which we weigh our own actions and the actions of all others. It is an innate part of our being, which to deny is to deny our own nature. When one child says to another, "You ought not do that," there has been an appeal to this common inherent rule of moral law. You may argue that no such law exists, but when you begin to have dealings with your fellowman you will expect him to conform to that commonly understood code.

• We are an unfaithful creation, and to compound our disobedience, rather than weep for our fallen state we turn to judge our Maker.

• The mark of universal sin is universal distrust of the Creator. The heavenly Father is not considered to be worthy of His children's confidence. It is no wonder that in Scripture the foundation for a restored relationship with God is *trust*. All relationships of any substance are built on trust.

• In answer to the question, "If God's goal was to have sons and daughters in His own image, why not create them as Himself, incapable of sinning?" we have seen that free will is an essential element of personhood. Man in God's image must have a free will. God has knowledge of good and evil, with commitment to the good. Whereas men, though as free as God, are born without character. We have gained knowledge of good and evil by plunging into the evil. We have developed negative character. Life on this earth is a moral incubator where we are to develop character like God's.

• The infinite God must have foreseen the ultimate outcome of setting in motion the possibilities that existed in a world of free-will creatures—six billion "gods" seeking their own.

• A God who has otherwise demonstrated Himself to be good should be given the benefit of the doubt. Not being able to see into the future, can we know that the outcome will not vindicate God's goodness? For a finite being to assume the moral high ground and persist in judging the Eternal is not warranted by the evidence. It is intellectual and moral suicide.

• Again we are faced with an either-or situation. Either God is not very wise to have created such a mess, or regardless of human suspicion to the contrary He is executing a plan of supreme importance. If God is no more than an all-powerful being with limited wisdom then the human race is suffering from His mistakes. But if God knows something we don't, something that He sees in the future, then with confidence we may assume that the outcome will be supremely worth the human and Divine suffering.

• Are you, like a runaway teenager, continuing to maintain an accusing distance from the Father? Have you troubled to look at the breach from God's perspective? Could it be that when properly understood He will stand out as eminently just, loving, and kind, while we are found to be the rebels?

• God's original purpose is His ultimate purpose. In eternity past, God counseled with Himself and determined His goals. He saw every day of future history more clearly than if it was prerecorded on a video. The means to arrive at His objective was all foreseen before the first square-inch of space was created. Nothing that has happened has caught Him by surprise. When Satan intercepted God's plan by seducing Eve into rebellion, the plan of God was not derailed. The groanings and travailings of the earth have not altered God's plan. The destination God originally charted is still His objective—sons and daughters in His own image with whom He can fellowship—a kingdom of love and creativity.

• Recognizing the presence of a plan of moral government, we judge ourselves in regard to our compliance with the nature and purposes of God, and we repent toward Him. We voluntarily trust Him. We believe Him. We come into moral partnership with God. We join Him in the creation of a divine family. We weigh the options and choose the righteousness for its own sake.

• God Himself became the substitute sinner. By faith He received our sin so that by faith we can receive His righteousness. He paid a debt He did not owe to purchase that which was already His. The left hand of mercy purchased from the right hand of justice. God was satisfied with His own offering. When we are satisfied, the fellowship begins.

- Paradise is not only restored, it is constructed from the ruins in a way that brings a strength of glory and beauty that could not otherwise have existed.

- God's plan would have been immediately served if the human race had obeyed; but as it is, God will make use of the moral rubble to build His kingdom even more glorious.

The artist

Day after day the people came by the outdoor studio to watch the famous artist chisel the stone. The rubble and waste grew to be much larger than the stone that remained. The spectators doubted the wisdom of such waste and exertion until the image began to take shape. When the graceful, delicate form finally stood alone, it was a glory and praise to the artist. No one remembered the chips that had fallen, and no one asked if it was worth it.

Parable of the Kingdom

On the distant past shores of eternity God first launched the ship of earth onto the sea of time. The course had long since been plotted. The first man was the captain and subsequent mankind was the crew. The ship's crew and occupants were immature and untried. Many of them would be born at sea. Most would never know of the commencement of the voyage. Some would come to deny it. His goal was the freedom of people, most of whom had not yet been in bondage. A slave purchased and then given his freedom is a far more faithful son than one born in the house. The ship's owner desired a community, a kingdom wherein love and creativity would abound.

Then the great granddaddy of all the ship's occupants was seduced into mutiny. As each new member was born, in time he too followed in rebellion. The ship was steered off course and the original destination was forgotten. Over the years many mutinies followed. Many different captains stood at the rudder guiding the ship. God, the shipbuilder and kingdom planner, found ways to occasionally communicate with one or the other of the ship's occupants. Word began to spread that He would one day establish His son as captain. Often those who brought this message of hope were silenced by death. Yet the rumor persisted that there were plans for a benevolent captaincy and, ultimately, a kingdom.

Those who have observed the ship with its occupants report that it still wanders at Sea, seemingly unpiloted. Reliable word from inside has it that the Captain-King is preparing for Himself a selected family. He promised to return to His captaincy at a time when He was least expected and to receive a number of the ship's occupants who have begun to love His appearing. Having gone ahead to prepare a place, He is preparing to take back his kingdom by force. The message is out. *"Repent, for the kingdom is at hand."*

Infiniteness Undefined

In the beginning God, and nothing else.
And yet everything—only in His mind.
From ancient days
Though nothing was old—nothing new.
No coming or going
No yesterday or tomorrow
Only now.
No options and nothing to chance—no risk.
Infiniteness undefined.
Space without dimension, time without succession,
Energy without matter,
Love without an object.
God alone
But not lonely.

— God is love and He gives it to whoever wants it ✝

Eternal silence shattered by words—the tools of the artist
Let there be, and there was.
Self-expression—a starry backdrop.
The first moment of time
The first movement.
Divine hands covered with dust,
A self-portrait in His image.
Love has an object
Of God, yet separate from,
Independent, but made to depend.
Free will, though not without cost
And the drama begins.

FREE NEWSLETTER

This book is made available to you as a ministry. The Pearls do not receive royalties on their books.

In response to the many questions we receive, we publish a monthly newsletter—**No Greater Joy**. It addresses the on-going issues of child training, marriage, and family. You can become a subscriber by simply sending us your name and address. If you have ordered materials directly from us, you will remain on our mailing list for one year. If you do not request the newsletter, after one year you will be cut from the mailing list.

If you are on our mailing list you will also receive notification of any seminars taught by the Pearls in your area.

If this book has been a blessing to you, why don't you do what many others are doing and bless your friends with a copy. If you order eight or more you will save nearly 40%.

Write today and receive a free subscription to our newsletter.

The Church At Cane Creek
1000 Pearl Road
Pleasantville, TN 37033
United States of America

FREE subscription to newsletter with order

Books by Michael & Debi Pearl

Order Form 1999

	Quan.	Code	Description		Suggested gift	Total
BOOKS					**EACH**	
		BK 9S	To Train Up A Child	1-7 books	4.00	
		BK 9X	To Train Up A Child	8-99 books	2.50	
		BK 9C	To Train Up A Child	Box of 100	2.20	
		BK 1S	No Greater Joy Volume One	1-7 books	4.00	
		BK 1X	No Greater Joy Volume One	8-99 books	2.50	
		BK 1C	No Greater Joy Volume One	Box of 100	2.20	
		BK R1	Rebekah's Diary	1-7 books	4.00	
		BK D1	By Divine Design	1-7 books	4.00	
		BK DX	By Divine Design	8-99 books	4.00	
		BK DC	By Divine Design	Box of 100	4.00	

The Church at Cane Creek
1000 Pearl Road
Pleasantville, TN 37033

Sub Total	
Postage	
Total	

Please print your name and address clearly.

You need not tear this out of your book. Just print your order clearly.